LITTLE PUFFERS

Britain's Great Little Trains

2024-2025

EDITOR
John Robinson

Sixteenth Edition

ACKNOWLEDGEMENTS

Following a 5-year hiatus which was caused mainly by the Covid pandemic lockdown and its aftermath, we are pleased now to re-launch Little Puffers as a separate publication following on from last year's partial re-launch when we included quite a number of narrow-gauge railways within the 2023-2024 edition of Still Steaming.

As always, we were greatly impressed by the friendly and cooperative manner of the staff and helpers of the railways which we selected to appear in this book, and wish to thank them all for the help they have given. In addition we wish to thank Bob Budd (cover design), Michael Robinson (page layouts) and Jonathan James (who provided a number of photographs) for their help.

Although we believe that the information contained in this guide is accurate at the time of going to press, we, and the Railways and Museums itemised, are unable to accept liability for any loss, damage, distress or injury suffered as a result of any inaccuracies. Furthermore, we and the Railways are unable to guarantee operating and opening times which may always be subject to cancellation without notice, particularly during adverse weather conditions.

If you feel we should include other locations or information in future editions, please let us know so that we may give them consideration. We would like to thank you for buying this guide and wish you 'Happy Railway Travelling'!

John Robinson

EDITOR

British Library Cataloguing in Publication Data
A catalogue record for this book is available from the British Library

ISBN-13:   978-1-86223-515-1

Copyright © 2024, SOCCER BOOKS LIMITED. (01472 696226)
72 St. Peter's Avenue, Cleethorpes, N.E. Lincolnshire, DN35 8HU, England

www.soccer-books.co.uk

Manufactured in the UK by 4edge Ltd

FOREWORD

For the purposes of this publication, we define railways solely by their gauge and include only those with a gauge in excess of 10 inches but less than UK Standard gauge. We also publish two other books: 'Still Steaming', covering Standard gauge railways and 'Tiny Trains', covering railways with gauges of 9½ inches and smaller. Both of these publications, as well as further copies of 'Little Puffers' can be ordered UK post free from the Soccer Books Limited address opposite or via our website: www.soccer-books.co.uk

The cover photograph was taken on the Lynton & Barnstaple Railway on 28th August 2020.

CONTENTS

ABBEY PUMPING STATION

Address: Abbey Pumping Station Museum, Corporation Road, Leicester, LE4 5PX **Telephone Nº:** (0116) 299-5111 **Year Formed:** 1974 **Location of Line:** Leicester **Length of Line:** 300 yards	**Nº of Steam Locos:** 1 **Nº of Other Locos:** 4 **Approx Nº of Visitors P.A.:** 60,000 **Gauge:** 2 feet **Website:** www.abbeypumpingstation.org

GENERAL INFORMATION

Nearest Mainline Station: Leicester London Road (3 miles)
Nearest Bus Station: Leicester (1½ miles)
Car Parking: Free parking available on site (£3.00 for parking at the Space Centre on Special Event days)
Coach Parking: Use the Space Centre car park
Souvenir Shop(s): Yes
Food & Drinks: Available on special event days only

SPECIAL INFORMATION

The Museum is situated in the Abbey Pumping Station which, from 1891 to 1964 pumped Leicester's sewage to nearby treatment works. The Museum now collects and displays the industrial, technological and scientific heritage of Leicester and contains rare working examples of Woolf compound rotative beam engines which are in steam on selected days.

OPERATING INFORMATION

Opening Times: The Pumping Station is open daily from February to October, 11.00am to 4.30pm, except for Special Event Days when times may vary. Trains run only on Special Event days.
Steam Working: Selected Special Event days only. Details are shown on the Museum's website three months in advance.
Prices: Admission to the museum is free of charge except for Special Event Days. Prices vary on these dates so please check the web site for further details.

Detailed Directions by Car:
From All Parts: The Museum is situated next to the National Space Centre, about 1 mile North of Leicester city centre near Beaumont Leys and Belgrave. Brown tourist signs with a distinctive rocket logo provide directions to the NSC from the arterial routes around Leicester and the Museum is nearby.

ALMOND VALLEY LIGHT RAILWAY

Address: Almond Valley Heritage Centre, Millfield, Livingston   EH54 7AR
Telephone Nº: (01506) 414957
Year Formed: 1993
Location of Line: Livingston
Length of Line: 550 yards

Nº of Steam Locos: None
Nº of Other Locos: 3
Approx Nº of Visitors P.A.: 125,000
Gauge: 2 feet 6 inches
Website: www.almondvalley.co.uk

GENERAL INFORMATION

Nearest Mainline Station: Livingston North (1 mile)
Nearest Bus Station: Livingston (1 mile)
Car Parking: Available on site
Coach Parking: Available
Souvenir Shop(s): Yes
Food & Drinks: Available

SPECIAL INFORMATION

The railway runs through the grounds of the Almond Valley Heritage Centre which hosts a wide range of other attractions including a farm, a historic Mill, nature trails and picnic areas.

OPERATING INFORMATION

Opening Times: The Centre is open daily from 10.00am to 5.00pm throughout the year except on 25th & 26th December and 1st & 2nd January. The railway operates at weekends between Easter and the end of September, and daily during some holiday periods, from 11.00am to 4.00pm. Please contact Almond Valley for further details.
Steam Working: None at present.
Prices: Adults £11.00 (Admission to Centre only)
Children £9.00 (Admission to Centre only)
Senior Citizen £10.00 (Admission only)
Note: Train rides are an extra £2.00 per person.

Detailed Directions by Car:
From All Parts: Exit the M8 at Junction 3A and take the A779 towards Livingston. Almond Valley Heritage Centre is located near the junction of the A779 and the A705 and is clearly signposted.

AMBERLEY MUSEUM

Address: Amberley Museum, New Barn Road, Amberley, Arundel BN18 9LT **Telephone Nº**: (01798) 831370 **Year Formed**: 1979 **Location of Line**: Amberley **Length of Line**: ¾ mile	**Nº of Steam Locos**: 3 **Nº of Other Locos**: 20+ **Approx Nº of Visitors P.A.**: 50,000 **Gauge**: 2 feet **Website**: www.amberleymuseum.co.uk **E-mail**: office@amberleymuseum.co.uk

GENERAL INFORMATION

Nearest Mainline Station: Amberley (adjacent)
Nearest Bus Station: –
Car Parking: Free parking available on site
Coach Parking: Free parking available on site
Souvenir Shop(s): Yes
Food & Drinks: Yes

SPECIAL INFORMATION

Amberley Museum covers 36 acres of former chalk pits and comprises over 40 buildings containing hundreds of different exhibits. There is plenty to see in all weathers and dogs are welcome.

OPERATING INFORMATION

Opening Times: 2024 dates: Wednesday to Sunday from 10th February to 3rd November and also on Bank Holiday Mondays. Trains operate from approximately 10.00am until 4.30pm.
The Museum itself is open from 10.00am to 4.30pm.
Steam Working: Most Sundays but please check the web site for full details.
Prices: Adult £17.00
    Child £7.50 (free for Under-5's)
    Concessions £15.00
    Families £30.00 to £45.00
    (depends on numbers of family members)

Detailed Directions by Car:
From All Parts: Amberley Museum is situated in West Sussex on the B2139 mid-way between Arundel and Storrington and is adjacent to Amberley Railway Station.

AMERTON RAILWAY

Address: Amerton Railway, Stow-by-Chartley, Staffordshire ST18 0LA	**Nº of Steam Locos:** 4
	Nº of Other Locos: 6 (+2 in restoration)
Telephone Nº: (01889) 271337	**Approx Nº of Visitors P.A.:** 30,000
Year Formed: 1991	**Gauge:** 2 feet
Location: Amerton Railway	**Website:** www.amertonrailway.co.uk
Length of Line: Approximately 1 mile	**E-mail:** enquiries@amertonrailway.co.uk

GENERAL INFORMATION

Nearest Mainline Station: Stafford (8 miles)
Nearest Bus Station: Stafford (8 miles)
Car Parking: Free parking available on site
Coach Parking: Available by arrangement
Souvenir Shop(s): Yes
Food & Drinks: Yes

SPECIAL INFORMATION

The railway operates both locomotives and rolling stock which were built in Staffordshire.

OPERATING INFORMATION

Opening Times: 2024 dates: Weekends and Bank Holidays from 27th March to 3rd November and Wednesdays during the School Summer Holidays. Santa Specials operate on weekends in December. Open from 11.30am to 4.30pm at weekends but only until 4.00pm during midweek dates.
Steam Working: Sundays and Bank Holidays
Prices: Adult £3.00
        Child £2.50
        Concession £2.50

Detailed Directions by Car:
Amerton is located on the A518, 1 mile from the junction with the A51 – Amerton Farm is signposted at the junction. The Railway is located approximately 8 miles from Junction 14 of the M6.

APEDALE VALLEY LIGHT RAILWAY

Address: Apedale Valley Country Park, Chesterton, Newcastle-under-Lyme
Telephone Nº: 0845 094-1953
Year Formed: 1969
Location: Apedale Valley Community Country Park
Length of Line: ¼ mile

Nº of Steam Locos: 4
Nº of Other Locos: 76
Gauge: 2 feet
Website: www.avlr.org.uk
E-mail: info@mrt.org.uk

GENERAL INFORMATION

Nearest Mainline Station: Longport (2 miles)
Nearest Bus Station: Hanley (3½ miles)
Car Parking: Available
Coach Parking: Available
Souvenir Shop(s): Yes
Food & Drinks: Available

SPECIAL INFORMATION

The Apedale Valley Light Railway is operated by the Moseley Railway Trust which plans to extend the line to over 1 mile in length.

OPERATING INFORMATION

Opening Times: 2024 dates: Every weekend and Bank Holiday from 30th March to 27th October. Santa Specials run on some December weekends. Trains usually run from 11.30am to 4.00pm. Please contact the railway or check the web site for further details.

Steam Working: Special Event days, Bank Holiday weekends plus the second weekend in each month.
Prices: Adult Return £4.00
　　　　　Child Return £2.00
　　　　　　Family Return £9.00
Note: Different prices may apply for special events.

Detailed Directions by Car:
Exit the M6 at Junction 16 and take the A500 to the A34 and head southwards. Turn right at the traffic island by the McDonald's restaurant and follow the brown tourist signs for Apedale Valley. Follow Loomer Road in Chesterton to the end and continue into the Park. Use the car park at the Heritage Centre as there is no direct access to the railway by car. SatNav: Use ST5 7LB. This postcode is the speedway track on the approach to the park. Continue past the speedway track and continue along Loomer Road for the park.

AUDLEY END STEAM RAILWAY

Address: Audley End, Saffron Walden, Essex CB11 4JB	**Nº of Steam Locos:** 5
Telephone Nº: (01799) 510726	**Nº of Other Locos:** 2
Year Formed: 1964	**Approx Nº of Visitors P.A.:** 42,000
Location of Line: Opposite Audley End House, Saffron Walden	**Gauge:** 10¼ inches
Length of Line: 1½ miles	**Website:** www.audley-end-railway.co.uk
	E-mail: enquiries@aemr.co.uk

GENERAL INFORMATION

Nearest Mainline Station: Audley End (1 mile)
Nearest Bus Station: Saffron Walden (1 mile)
Car Parking: Available on site
Coach Parking: Available on site
Souvenir Shop(s): Yes
Food & Drinks: Available in the Cafe

SPECIAL INFORMATION

Audley End Steam Railway is Lord Braybrooke's private miniature railway situated just next to Audley End House, an English Heritage site. Private parties can be catered for outside of normal running hours.

OPERATING INFORMATION

Opening Times: 2024 dates: Weekends and Bank Holidays from 16th March to 28th September, daily from 6th July to 8th September and also during other School Holidays.
Santa Specials operate at the end of November and in December. Trains run from 10.30pm until 3.30pm except on Special Event days.
Please check the web site for further information.
Steam Working: Most operating days.
Prices: Adult £8.00
Child £4.00 to £8.00 (depends on height)
Note: Different prices may apply for Special Events.

Detailed Directions by Car:
Exit the M11 at Junction 10 if southbound or Junction 9 if northbound and follow the signs for Audley End House. The railway is situated just across the road from Audley End House.

BALA LAKE RAILWAY

Address: Bala Lake Railway, Llanuwchllyn, Gwynedd, LL23 7DD	**Nº of Steam Locos:** 7 (6 in service)
Telephone Nº: (01678) 540666	**Nº of Other Locos:** 6
Year Formed: 1972	**Approx Nº of Visitors P.A.:** 26,000
Location of Line: Llanuwchllyn to Bala	**Gauge:** 1 foot 11 five-eighth inches
Length of Line: 4½ miles	**Website:** www.bala-lake-railway.co.uk
	E-mail: enquiries@bala-lake-railway.co.uk

GENERAL INFORMATION

Nearest Mainline Station: Wrexham (40 miles)
Nearest Bus Station: Wrexham (40 miles)
Car Parking: Adequate parking in Llanuwchllyn
Coach Parking: At Llanuwchllyn or in Bala Town Centre
Souvenir Shop(s): Yes
Food & Drinks: Yes – unlicensed!

SPECIAL INFORMATION

Bala Lake Railway is a narrow-gauge railway which follows 4½ miles of the former Ruabon to Barmouth G.W.R. line. Funds are being raised as part of the Red Dragon Project to extend the railway to Bala Town Station in Bala itself.

OPERATING INFORMATION

Opening Times: 2024 dates: 23rd March to 29th September but closed on Mondays and Fridays in April, May, June and September (except for Bank Holidays and during the School Holidays).
Also open on some dates during October.
Steam Working: All advertised services are steam hauled. Trains run from 10.10am to 6.20pm.
Prices: Adult Single £11.00; Return £16.00
Child Single £5.50; Return £7.50
Concession Return £15.00
Family Ticket: £18.50 (1 Adult + 1 Child)
Family Ticket: £37.00 (2 Adult + 2 Child)
Additional Children are then charged £4.50 each.
Under-3s travel free of charge.
Dogs travel for £1.00 (Guide dogs free of charge)

Detailed Directions by Car:
From All Parts: The railway is situated ½ mile off the A494 Bala to Dolgellau road which is accessible from the A470 and via the national motorway network. Follow the brown tourist signs from Llanuwchllyn or Bala.

BEALE RAILWAY

Address: Beale Wildlife Park, Lower
Basildon, Pangbourne   RG8 9NH
Telephone Nº: 0870 777-7160
Year Formed: 1989
Location of Line: Pangbourne, Berks.
Length of Line: Approximately 1 mile

Nº of Steam Locos: None
Nº of Other Locos: 1
Gauge: 10¼ inches
Website: www.bealepark.org.uk
E-mail: admin@bealepark.org.uk

GENERAL INFORMATION

Nearest Mainline Station: Pangbourne (1 mile)
Nearest Bus Station: Reading (12 miles)
Car Parking: Available on site
Coach Parking: Available on site
Souvenir Shop(s): Yes
Food & Drinks: Available

SPECIAL INFORMATION

The railway is situated within Child-Beale Trust,
Beale Park alongside the River Thames. The Park has
numerous other attractions including collections of
small exotic animals, farm animals & birds,
landscaped gardens & woodlands and play areas.

OPERATING INFORMATION

Opening Times: Beale Park is open daily from
10.00am to 5.00pm from October to March inclusive
and until 6.00pm at other times. The first train
departs at 10.30am daily and the last train departs
15 minutes before Beale Park closes.
Steam Working: Trains are now diesel operated.
Prices: One free ride is included in the park
admission fee. All rides thereafter are £1.00 each.
Park Admission: Adults £15.50
                      Children £13.50 (free Under-2s)
                      Concessions £14.50
Note: Visitors are encouraged to make a voluntary
donation so that Gift Aid can be claimed by the park.

Detailed Directions by Car:
Beale Park is situated just off the A329 Reading to Goring Road at Pangbourne.

BICKINGTON STEAM RAILWAY

Address: Trago Mills Shopping & Leisure Centre, Stover, Devon   TQ12 6JB
Telephone Nº: (01626) 821111
Year Formed: 1988
Location of Line: Near the junction of A38 and A382

Nº of Steam Locos: 4
Nº of Other Locos: 1
Approx Nº of Visitors P.A.: Not known
Gauge: 10¼ inches
Length of Line: 2½ miles

GENERAL INFORMATION

Nearest Mainline Station: Newton Abbott (3½ miles)
Nearest Bus Station: Newton Abbott
Car Parking: Free parking available on site
Coach Parking: Available on site
Souvenir Shop(s): Yes
Food & Drinks: Available adjacent to the Railway

SPECIAL INFORMATION

Bickington Steam Railway is part of the Trago Mills Shopping & Leisure Centre. The site has numerous other attractions including, 'The Finest 00-gauge Model Railway in the UK'!

OPERATING INFORMATION

Opening Times: 2024: Weekends and Bank Holidays throughout the year then daily from the last week of May to the last week of September and during other School Holidays.
Also open for Santa Specials in December.
Trains run from 11.00am on operating days.
Steam Working: Most operating days but please contact the Railway for precise information.
Prices: Adults £3.00
Children £2.00 (Under-4s free)
Concessions £2.00

Detailed Directions by Car:
From All Parts: Take the M5 from Exeter to the A38 and head towards Plymouth. Exit at the junction with the A382 and follow the signs for 'Trago Mills'. The railway is approximately 1 mile. (SatNav use TQ12 6JD)

BICTON WOODLAND RAILWAY

Address: Bicton Woodland Railway, Bicton Park Botanical Gardens, East Budleigh, Budleigh Salterton   EX9 7OP
Telephone Nº: (01395) 568465
Year Formed: 1963
Location of Line: Bicton Gardens
Length of Line: 1½ miles

Nº of Steam Locos: None at present
Nº of Other Locos: 2
Approx Nº of Visitors P.A.: 300,000
Gauge: 1 foot 6 inches
Website: www.bictongardens.co.uk

GENERAL INFORMATION

Nearest Railtrack Station: Exmouth (6 miles)
Nearest Bus Station: Exeter (14 miles)
Car Parking: Free parking at site
Coach Parking: Free parking at site
Souvenir Shop(s): Yes
Food & Drinks: Yes

SPECIAL INFORMATION

The railway runs through the grounds of Bicton Park Botanical Gardens which span over 60 acres. The railway is the only 18 inch gauge line in the UK.

OPERATING INFORMATION

Opening Times: Daily from 10.00am to 5.30pm during the Summer months and 10.00am to 4.30pm during the Winter.
Closed on Christmas Day and Boxing Day.
Steam Working: None at present
Prices: Adult £14.50 (Entrance);   £4.00 (Rides)
Child £11.50 (Entrance);   £2.50 (Rides)
Concessions £12.50 (Entrance);   £3.50 (Rides)
Note: Under-2s ride for free and entrance tickets for the gardens are cheaper when purchased online.

Detailed Directions by Car:
From All Parts: Exit the M5 motorway at Exeter services, Junction 30 and follow the brown tourist signs to Bicton Park.   For SATNAV to the railway, please use the following postcode: EX9 7BG

BRECON MOUNTAIN RAILWAY

Address: Pant Station, Merthyr Tydfil, CF48 2DD
Telephone Nº: (01685) 722988
Year Formed: 1980
Location of Line: North of Merthyr Tydfil – 1 mile from the A465
Length of Line: 5 miles

Gauge: 1 foot 11¾ inches
Nº of Steam Locos: 7
Nº of Other Locos: 3
Approx Nº of Visitors P.A.: 75,000
Website: www.bmr.wales
E-mail: enquiries@bmr.wales

GENERAL INFORMATION

Nearest Mainline Station: Merthyr Tydfil (3 miles)
Nearest Bus Station: Merthyr Tydfil (3 miles)
Car Parking: Free parking available at Pant Station
Coach Parking: Free parking available at Pant Station
Souvenir Shop(s): Yes
Food & Drinks: Yes – including licensed Tea Rooms

SPECIAL INFORMATION

It is possible to take a break before the return journey at Pontsticill to have a picnic, take a forest walk, visit the lakeside snackbar and play area or visit the new Steam Museum.

OPERATING INFORMATION

Opening Times: 2024 dates: Daily from 23rd March to 27th October except for Fridays and most Mondays. Trains typically run from 10.30am to 3.45pm at peak times and from 10.30pm to 2.30pm during off-peak times.
Steam Working: Most services are steam hauled.
Prices: Adults Return £22.00
Children Return £11.00 (Under-2s free)

Detailed Directions by Car:
Exit the M4 at Junction 32 and take the A470 to Merthyr Tydfil. Go onto the A465 and follow the brown tourist signs for the railway. SATNAV users should enter the following postcode: CF48 2DD

BREDGAR & WORMSHILL LIGHT RAILWAY

Address: The Warren, Bredgar, near Sittingbourne, Kent ME9 8AT **Telephone Nº:** (01622) 884254 **Year Formed:** 1972 **Location of Line:** 1 mile south of Bredgar **Length of Line:** ¾ mile	**Gauge:** 2 feet **Nº of Steam Locos:** 8 **Nº of Other Locos:** 5 **Approx Nº of Visitors P.A.:** 7,000 **Website:** www.bwlr.co.uk **E-mail:** info@bwlr.co.uk

GENERAL INFORMATION

Nearest Mainline Station: Sittingbourne (5 miles)
Nearest Bus Station: Sittingbourne
Car Parking: 500 spaces available – free parking
Coach Parking: Free parking available by appointment
Souvenir Shop(s): Yes
Food & Drinks: Yes

SPECIAL INFORMATION

A small but beautiful railway in rural Kent. The railway also has other attractions including a Model Railway, Traction Engines, a Beam Engine, Vintage cars and tractors, a Locomotive Shed, a picnic site and woodland walks.

OPERATING INFORMATION

Opening Times: 2024 dates: Open on Easter Sunday then the first Sunday of the month from May to October and also on Sunday 27th October. Trains run from 11.00am to 4.30pm.
Steam Working: Every operating day.
Prices: Adult £20.00
              Child £10.00 (Under-4s travel free)
              Family Ticket £50.00
                            (2 adults + 3 children)
Note: The prices shown above include parking and unlimited rides on the day of purchase. Tickets purchased in advance are much cheaper.

Detailed Directions by Car:
Take the M20 and exit at Junction 8 (Leeds Castle exit). Travel 4½ miles due north through Hollingbourne. The Railway is situated a little over 1 mile south of Bredgar village.

BURE VALLEY RAILWAY

Address: Aylsham Station, Norwich Road, Aylsham, Norfolk NR11 6BW	**Nº of Steam Locos:** 5
Telephone Nº: (01263) 733858	**Nº of Other Locos:** 3
Year Formed: 1989	**Approx Nº of Visitors P.A.:** 120,000
Location of Line: Aylsham to Wroxham	**Gauge:** 15 inches
Length of Line: 9 miles	**Website:** www.bvrw.co.uk
	E-mail: info@bvrw.co.uk

GENERAL INFORMATION

Nearest Mainline Station: Hoveton & Wroxham (adjacent)
Nearest Bus Station: Aylsham (bus passes station)
Car Parking: Free parking for passengers at Aylsham and Wroxham Stations
Coach Parking: As above
Souvenir Shop(s): Yes at both Stations
Food & Drinks: Yes (Café at Aylsham opens daily)

SPECIAL INFORMATION

Boat trains connect at Wroxham with a 1½ hour cruise on the Norfolk Broads National Park. Steam Locomotive driving courses are available throughout the year except in July and August. All trains have carriages which are able to carry wheelchairs.

OPERATING INFORMATION

Opening Times: Aylsham Station is open daily. Trains run on various dates in 2024 including weekends in February and daily from 23rd March to 3rd November, plus some other dates. Trains run from 10.00am to 5.25pm during high season. Open for Festive Express rides on weekends and other dates in November and December.
Steam Working: Most trains are steam-hauled
Prices: Adult Return £22.00
         Child Return £11.00
         Family Return £55.00 (2 adult + 2 child)
Note: An extra charge is made for Dogs and bicycles.

Detailed Directions by Car:
From Norwich: Aylsham Station is situated midway between Norwich and Cromer on the A140 – follow the signs for Aylsham Town Centre. Wroxham Station is adjacent to the Wroxham British Rail Station – take the A1151 from Norwich; From King's Lynn: Take the A148 and B1354 to reach Aylsham Station.
Satellite Navigation: Use NR11 6BW for Aylsham Station and NR12 8UU for Wroxham Station.

BURSLEDON BRICKWORKS MUSEUM

Address: Swanwick Lane, Swanwick, Southampton SO31 7HB
Telephone No: (01489) 576248
Year Formed: 1994 (Railway established in 2010)
Location of Line: Bursledon Brickworks
Length of Line: A third of a mile

No of Steam Locos: 2
No of Other Locos: 2
Approx No of Visitors P.A.: 8,000
Gauge: 2 feet and 7¼ inches
Website: www.thebrickmusem.org

GENERAL INFORMATION

Nearest Mainline Station: Bursledon (¾ mile)
Nearest Bus Station: Southampton
Car Parking: Available on site
Coach Parking: Available on site
Souvenir Shop(s): On site
Food & Drinks: Available

SPECIAL INFORMATION

The 2 foot gauge railway is operated by the Hampshire Narrow Gauge Railway Trust which owns 2 steam locomotives and 2 heritage petrol-driven locomotives.

OPERATING INFORMATION

Opening Times: 2024 dates: Wednesdays, Thursdays and Sundays from 3rd April to 3rd November. Open 11.00am to 4.00pm.
Steam Working: Please check the web site for details
Prices: Adults £57.00 (£9.50 Special Event days)
  Children £5.00 (£7.50 Steam Event days)
  Concessions £6.00 (£8.50 Event days)
  Family £21.00 (£29.00 Special Events)
Note: There is a small additional charge for train rides which are subject to availability.

Detailed Directions by Car:
Exit the M27 at Junction 8 and take the A3024 towards Bursledon. Take the first exit at the roundabout onto the A27 Bridge Road, passing Bursledon on the right before turning left into Swanwick Lane after crossing the River Hamble. The Brickworks is on the left from Swanwick Lane, situated alongside the M27.

CLEETHORPES COAST LIGHT RAILWAY

Address: Lakeside Station, King's Road, Cleethorpes, DN35 0AG
Telephone Nº: (01472) 604657
Year Formed: 1948
Location of Line: Lakeside Park & Marine embankment along Cleethorpes seafront
Length of Line: 2 miles (not all in use)

Nº of Steam Locos: 3
Nº of Other Locos: 5
Gauge: 15 inches
Website: www.cclr.co.uk
E-mail: info@cclr.co.uk

GENERAL INFORMATION

Nearest Mainline Station: Cleethorpes (1 mile)
Nearest Bus Stop: Meridian Point (opposite)
Car Parking: Boating Lake car park is adjacent – 500 spaces (fee charged)
Coach Parking: As above
Souvenir Shop(s): Yes
Food & Drinks: Sidings Snack Shack and The Signal Box Inn, described as 'The Smallest Pub on the Planet', are both located at Lakeside Station.

OPERATING INFORMATION

Opening Times: 2024 dates: Open weekends and School Holidays throughout the year and daily from 23rd March to 3rd November.
Santa Specials operate on weekends in December.
Trains run from 10.30am on most days.
Please check the website for further details.
Steam Working: Mostly weekends & Bank Holidays
Prices: Adult Return £5.49
　　　　　 Child Return £4.99
　　　　　 Single Journey £3.99
　　　　　 Dogs £1.50
Note: Card payments only – cash is not accepted.

Detailed Directions by Car:
Take the M180 to the A180 and continue to its' end. Follow signs for Cleethorpes. The Railway is situated along Cleethorpes seafront 1 mile to the south of the Pier. Look for the brown tourist signs marked Meridian Lakeside and the main station is adjacent to the Leisure Centre.

THE CORRIS RAILWAY

Address: Station Yard, Corris, Machynlleth, Mid Wales SY20 9SH
Telephone Nº: (01654) 761303
Year Formed: 1966
Location of Line: Corris to Maespoeth, Mid Wales
Length of Line: ¾ mile

Nº of Steam Locos: 1
Nº of Other Locos: 5
Approx Nº of Visitors P.A.: 7,000
Gauge: 2 feet 3 inches
Website: www.corris.co.uk
E-mail: enquiries@corris.co.uk

GENERAL INFORMATION

Nearest Mainline Station: Machynlleth (5 miles)
Nearest Bus Station: Machynlleth (5 miles)
Car Parking: Available on site and also at the Corris Craft Centre (500 yards)
Coach Parking: Corris Craft Centre (please pre-book if visiting)
Souvenir Shop(s): Yes
Food & Drinks: Yes

SPECIAL INFORMATION

The Corris Railway originally ran from 1859 to 1948. A second steam locomotive and two carriages are being built and work on an extension to the partly-rebuilt line is currently underway.

OPERATING INFORMATION

Opening Times: 2024 dates: The railway operates at weekends, during School Holidays and on Bank Holidays and some other dates between 29th March and 26th October.
Santa Specials run on 7th & 8th December.
The first train leaves Corris Station at 11.00am, the last train leaves at 3.30pm.
Steam Working: Most trains are steam-hauled.
Prices: Adult Return £8.00
 Child Return £4.00 (Ages 5 to 15)
 Family Return £20.00
  (2 adults + 2 children)

Detailed Directions by Car:
From All Parts: Corris is situated off the A487, five miles north of Machynlleth and 11 miles south of Dolgellau. Turn off the trunk road at the Braichgoch Bunkhouse & Inn and the Station Yard is the 2nd turning on the right as you enter the village, just past the Holy Trinity Church.

CROWLE PEATLAND RAILWAY

Address: The Old Peatworks, Dole Road, Crowle, DN17 4BL
Telephone Nº: (07739) 921835
Year Formed: 2013 (opened 2020)
Location of Line: Old Peatworks to Turf Moor Halt
Length of Line: 500 Metres

Nº of Steam Locos: None
Nº of Other Locos: 7 (+ Lisbon Tram)
Approx Nº of Visitors P.A.: 3,000
Gauge: 3-Foot
Website: www.peatland.co.uk
E-mail: admin@peatland.co.uk

GENERAL INFORMATION

Nearest Mainline Station: Crowle (½ mile)
Car Parking: Available on site
Coach Parking: Available on site
Food & Drinks: The Moorside Cafe is on site

SPECIAL INFORMATION

The site was operated as a Horse-drawn Railway until the 1960s! Unusual Schoma Locomotives are currently on site as well as Lisbon Tram No. 711.

OPERATING INFORMATION

Opening Times: 2024 dates: 30th & 31st March then the 2nd weekend of each month throughout the year.
Steam Working: None
Prices: Adult Return £2.00
           Child Return £1.00
Note: Higher prices may apply for Special Events.

Detailed Directions by Car: Exit the M180 at junction 2 and follow the A161 towards Goole for Crowle. Upon reaching the Crowle turn-off take the high-level road into Crowle and, after crossing over the railway line and canal, follow the Brown Duck Signs. The railway is outside of the village along Moor Road and Dole Road.

DEVON RAILWAY CENTRE

Address: The Station, Bickleigh, Tiverton, EX16 8RG	**N⁰ of Steam Locos:** 1
Telephone N⁰: (01884) 855671	**N⁰ of Other Locos:** 12
Year Formed: 1997	**Approx N⁰ of Visitors P.A.:** Not recorded
Location of Line: Bickleigh, Devon	**Gauge:** 2 feet, 7¼ inches and Standard
Length of Line: ½ mile (2 foot and 7¼ inch gauges); 200 yards (Standard gauge)	**Website:** www.devonrailwaycentre.co.uk
	E-mail: devonrailway@btinternet.com

GENERAL INFORMATION

Nearest Mainline Station: Exeter
Nearest Bus Station: Tiverton (Route 55)
Car Parking: Available on site
Coach Parking: Available on site
Souvenir Shop(s): Yes
Food & Drinks: Yes

SPECIAL INFORMATION

Devon Railway Centre has passenger-carrying lines and also features a large model railway exhibition with 15 working layouts. A delightful Edwardian model village built to a 1:12 scale has recently been extended with a model funfair added and a new museum coach is also available.

OPERATING INFORMATION

Opening Times: 2024 dates: Daily from 29th March to 14th April, then all weekends from 20th April to 3rd October. Also open on Thursdays and Fridays from 2nd May to 29th September and Tuesdays and Wednesdays in July and August. Open from 10.30am until 5.00pm on all operating days.
Steam Working: Please check web site for details.
Prices: Adult £12.80   Child £11.80
          Senior Citizen £12.30
          Family £47.90 to £58.00 (Under-3s free)
Admission includes unlimited train rides and access to the model village, model railways, museum and crazy golf.

Detailed Directions by Car:
From All Parts: Devon Railway Centre is situated adjacent to the famous Bickleigh Bridge, just off the A396 Exeter to Tiverton road (3 miles from Tiverton and 8 miles from Exeter).

EASTLEIGH LAKESIDE STEAM RAILWAY

Address: Lakeside Country Park,
Wide Lane, Eastleigh, Hants. SO50 5PE
Telephone Nº: (023) 8061-2020
Year Formed: 1992
Location: Opposite Southampton airport
Length of Line: 1¼ miles

Nº of Steam Locos: 21
Nº of Other Locos: 3
Approx Nº of Visitors P.A.: 50,000
Gauge: 10¼ inches and 7¼ inches
Website: www.steamtrain.co.uk
E-mail: elr@steamtrain.co.uk

GENERAL INFORMATION

Nearest Mainline Station: Southampton Airport (Parkway) (¼ mile)
Nearest Bus Station: Eastleigh (1½ miles)
Car Parking: Free parking available on site
Coach Parking: Free parking available on site
Souvenir Shop(s): Yes
Food & Drinks: Cafe on site is open all year round from 9.00am to 4.00pm.

SPECIAL INFORMATION

The railway also has a playground and picnic area overlooking the lakes.

OPERATING INFORMATION

Opening Times: Weekends throughout the year and daily during the school holidays. Open 10.00am to 4.30pm (until 4.00pm during the winter months).
Steam Working: As above
Prices: Adult Return £4.60 (First Class £5.10)
Child Return £3.60 (First Class £4.10)
Tickets are available offering 3 return journeys at reduced rates. Annual season tickets are available. Children under the age of 2 years ride free of charge. Driver training courses can be booked in advance.

Detailed Directions by Car:
From All Parts: Exit the M27 at Junction 5 and take the A335 to Eastleigh. The Railway is situated ¼ mile past Southampton Airport Station on the left hand side of the A335.

EAST SUFFOLK LIGHT RAILWAY

Address: East Anglia Transport Museum,
Chapel Road, Carlton Colville,
Lowestoft NR33 8BL
Telephone Nº: (01502) 518459
Year Formed: 1972
Location: 3 miles south of Lowestoft
Length of Line: 200 yards

Nº of Steam Locos: None
Nº of Other Locos: 4
Approx Nº of Visitors P.A.: 18,000
Gauge: 2 feet
Website: www.eatransportmuseum.co.uk

GENERAL INFORMATION

Nearest Mainline Station: Oulton Broad South
(2 miles)
Nearest Bus Station: Lowestoft (3 miles)
Car Parking: Available on site
Coach Parking: Available
Souvenir Shop(s): Yes
Food & Drinks: Available

SPECIAL INFORMATION

The railway is located at the East Anglia Transport
Museum which also offers visitors trolleybus and
tram rides.

OPERATING INFORMATION

Opening Times: 2024 dates: Sundays, Bank
Holidays and Thursdays from 29th March to 31st
October, Tuesdays from 7th May to 27th August and
some other dates. Usually open from 12.00pm to
4.30pm except for Special Event days.
Please check the web site for further information.
Steam Working: None
Prices: Adults £12.00 (Admission and all rides)
Children £6.00 (Admission and all rides)
(Under-5s ride free of charge)
Concessions £10.00 (Admission and rides)

Detailed Directions by Car:
From All Parts: The East Anglia Transport Museum is clearly signposted by brown tourist signs from the A12,
A146, A1117 and A1145.

EVESHAM VALE LIGHT RAILWAY

Address: The Valley, Evesham WR11 4DS	**Nº of Steam Locos:** 3
Telephone Nº: (01386) 422282	**Nº of Other Locos:** 2
Year Formed: 2002	**Approx Nº of Visitors P.A.:** 50,000
Location of Line: 1 mile north of Evesham	**Gauge:** 15 inches
Length of Line: 1¼ miles	**Website:** www.eveshamvalelightrailway.co.uk
	E-mail: enquiries@evlr.co.uk

GENERAL INFORMATION

Nearest Mainline Station: Evesham (1 mile)
Nearest Bus Station: Evesham (1½ miles)
Car Parking: Available in the Country Park
Coach Parking: Available in the Country Park
Souvenir Shop(s): Yes
Food & Drinks: Various restaurants and cafés in the shopping area.

SPECIAL INFORMATION

The railway is situated within the 130 acre Evesham Country Park which has apple orchards and picnic areas overlooking the picturesque Vale of Evesham.

OPERATING INFORMATION

Opening Times: Open at weekends throughout the year and daily during the school holidays. Trains run from 10.30am to 4.30pm. Please phone for further details.
Steam Working: Daily when trains are running.
Prices: Adult Return £3.30
Child Return £2.70 (Aged 2-15)
Note: Special reduced party rates are available for groups of 20 or more when booked in advance and Christmas specials operate during December.

Detailed Directions by Car:
From the North: Exit the M42 at Junction 3 and take the A435 towards Alcester then the A46 to Evesham; From the South: Exit the M5 at Junction 9 and take the A46 to Evesham; From the West: Exit the M5 at Junction 7 and take the A44 to Evesham; From the East: Take the A44 from Oxford to Evesham. Upon reaching Evesham, follow the Brown tourist signs for Evesham Country Park and the railway.

EXBURY GARDENS RAILWAY

Address: Exbury Gardens, Exbury, Near Southampton SO45 1AZ **Telephone Nº:** (02380) 891203 **Year Formed:** 2001 **Location of Line:** Exbury **Length of Line:** 1½ miles	**Nº of Steam Locos:** 3 **Nº of Other Locos:** 1 **Approx Nº of Visitors P.A.:** 85,000 **Gauge:** 12¼ inches **Website:** www.exbury.co.uk

Photograph courtesy of Gavin Clinton

GENERAL INFORMATION

Nearest Mainline Station: Brockenhurst (8 miles)
Nearest Bus Station: Hill Top (2½ miles)
The New Forest Open Tour Bus visits the gardens 8 times a day between 8th July and 10th September.
Car Parking: Free parking available on site
Coach Parking: Free parking available on site
Souvenir Shop(s): Yes
Food & Drinks: Available

SPECIAL INFORMATION

The railway is located in the world famous Rothschild azalea and rhododendron gardens at Exbury in the New Forest. A walk-through exhibition in the Engine Shed recalls the building of the steam railway.

OPERATING INFORMATION

Opening Times: 2024 dates: Daily from the 9th March to 3rd November. The gardens are open from 10.00am to 5.00pm (or dusk if earlier) and car park gates close at 6.00pm.
Steam Working: Most running days from 11.00am (restricted operation in March and September).
Prices: Adult £16.00 (Plus £6.50 for train tickets)
      Child £6.00 (Plus £6.50 for train tickets)
      (Under-3s ride free of charge)
Note: The above prices are admission to the Gardens which is required to visit the railway. Train rides are £6.50 extra as above.

Detailed Directions by Car:
From all directions: Exit the M27 at Junction 2 and take the A326 to Dibden. Follow the brown tourist signs for Exbury Gardens & Steam Railway.

FAIRBOURNE RAILWAY

Address: Beach Road, Fairbourne, Dolgellau, Gwynedd LL38 2EX	**Nº of Steam Locos:** 4
Telephone Nº: (01341) 250362	**Nº of Other Locos:** 2
Year Formed: 1916	**Approx Nº of Visitors P.A.:** 18,000
Location of Line: On A493 between Tywyn & Dolgellau	**Gauge:** 12¼ inches
Length of Line: 2 miles	**Website:** www.fairbournerailway.com
	E-mail: office@fairbournerailway.com

GENERAL INFORMATION

Nearest Mainline Station: Fairbourne (adjacent)
Nearest Bus Station: Fairbourne (adjacent)
Car Parking: Available in Mainline station car park
Coach Parking: Pay & Display car park 300 yards
Souvenir Shop(s): Yes
Food & Drinks: Yes – licensed Cafes at Fairbourne and Barmouth Ferry Terminus

SPECIAL INFORMATION

There is a connecting ferry service (foot passengers only) from Barmouth to Barmouth Ferry Terminus.

OPERATING INFORMATION

Opening Times: 2024 dates: Open daily from 23rd March until 3rd November but closed on Mondays and Fridays except during the School Holidays. Santa Specials usually run on a weekend in December.
Steam Working: The majority of services are steam-hauled. A special Steam Gala runs on 27th, 28th and 29th May.
Prices: Adult Day Rover £13.75
Unaccompanied Child Day Rover £8.00
(accompanied Children – £1.00 each)
Under-3s ride for free
Dog ticket £1.00

Detailed Directions by Car:
From A470: Follow signs for Dolgellau and turn left onto A493 towards Tywyn. The turn-off for Fairbourne is located 8 miles south-west of Dolgellau; From South Wales: Follow signs for Machynlleth, then follow A487 towards Dolgellau. Then take A493 towards Fairbourne.

FERRY MEADOWS MINIATURE RAILWAY

Address: Ham Lane, Nene Park,
Oundle Road, Peterborough   PE2 5UU
Telephone Nº: (01933) 398889
Year Formed: 1978
Location: Ferry Meadows, Nene Park
Length of Line: ½ mile

Nº of Steam Locos: 1
Nº of Other Locos: 2
Approx Nº of Visitors P.A.: 55,000
Gauge: 10¼ inches
Website: www.ferrymeadowsrailway.co.uk

GENERAL INFORMATION

Nearest Mainline Station: Peterborough (2 miles)
Nearest Bus Station: Peterborough (2 miles)
Car Parking: Available adjacent
Coach Parking: Available adjacent
Souvenir Shop(s): Yes
Food & Drinks: Available

SPECIAL INFORMATION

The railway is situated in the Ferry Meadows area of
Nene Park in which watersports and other leisure
activities are also available.

OPERATING INFORMATION

Opening Times: 2024 dates: Every weekend and
Bank Holiday throughout the year and daily during
School Holidays.
Trains run from 11.30am to 4.30pm.
Steam Working: Every Sunday and some weekdays
during the School Holidays.
Please contact the railway for further details.
Prices: Adult Return £3.00   Adult Single £2.00
          Child Return £3.00   Child Single £2.00

Detailed Directions by Car:
Nene Park is situated on the A605 Oundle Road. Follow the brown tourist signs for Nene Park.

FFESTINIOG RAILWAY

Address: Ffestiniog Railway, Harbour
Station, Porthmadog, Gwynedd LL49 9NF
Telephone Nº: (01766) 516000
Year Formed: 1832
Location of Line: Porthmadog to
Blaenau Ffestiniog
Length of Line: 13½ miles

Nº of Steam Locos: 12
Nº of Other Locos: 12
Approx Nº of Visitors P.A.: 360,000
Gauge: 1 foot 11½ inches
Website: www.festrail.co.uk
E-mail: enquiries@ffwhr.com

GENERAL INFORMATION

Nearest Mainline Station: Blaenau Ffestiniog
(interchange) or Minffordd
Nearest Bus Station: Bus stop next to stations at
Porthmadog & Blaenau Ffestiniog
Car Parking: Parking available at Porthmadog,
Blaenau Ffestiniog, Minffordd and Tan-y-Bwlch
Coach Parking: Available at Porthmadog and
Blaenau Ffestiniog
Souvenir Shop(s): Yes   **Food & Drinks:** Yes

SPECIAL INFORMATION

The Railway runs through the spectacular scenery of
Snowdonia National Park and the line now links up
with the Welsh Highland Railway.

OPERATING INFORMATION

Opening Times: 2024 dates: Daily service from
29th March to 3rd November. A limited service also
operates during the Winter months and Santa
Specials run on dates during December.
Please check the web site for further information.
Steam Working: Most trains are steam hauled.
Prices: A variety of routes between Blaenau
Ffestiniog, Porthmadog and Caernarfon are
available following the link-up with the Welsh
Highland Railway, so please check the website for
full details of the various fares.

Detailed Directions by Car:
Portmadog is easily accessible from the Midlands – take the M54/A5 to Corwen then the A494 to Bala onto the
A4212 to Trawsfynydd and the A470 (becomes the A487 from Maentwrog) to Porthmadog. From Chester take
the A55 to Llandudno Junction and the A470 to Blaenau Ffestiniog. Both Stations are well-signposted.

GARTELL LIGHT RAILWAY

Address: Common Lane, Yenston,
Templecombe, Somerset   BA8 0NB
Telephone Nº: (01963) 370752
Year Formed: 1991
Location of Line: South of Templecombe
Length of Line: ¾ mile

Nº of Steam Locos: 2
Nº of Other Locos: 3
Approx Nº of Visitors P.A.: 3,000
Gauge: 2 feet
Website: www.newglr.weebly.com

GENERAL INFORMATION

Nearest Mainline Station: Templecombe (1¼ miles)
Nearest Bus Station: Wincanton
Car Parking: Free parking adjacent to the station
Coach Parking: Adjacent to the station
Souvenir Shop(s): Yes
Food & Drinks: Meals, snacks and drinks available

SPECIAL INFORMATION

Privately owned by the Gartell Family,the railway is
only open to the public on the days shown opposite.
Part of the line runs along the track bed of the
former Somerset & Dorset Joint Railway.

OPERATING INFORMATION

Opening Times: 2024 dates: 1st April; 6th May;
27th May; 30th June; 28th July; 26th August;
29th September and 27th October.
Trains depart at 25 minute intervals between
10.30am and 4.20pm.
Steam Working: Every operating day.
Prices: Adult £9.00
         Concession £8.00
         Child £5.00 (Ages 4 to 13)
         Family £22.00 (2 adults + 2 children)
Note: The railway is privately operated by the
Gartell Family & friends.

Detailed Directions by Car:
From All Parts: The Railway is situated off the A357 just south of Templecombe and on open days is clearly
indicated by the usual brown tourist signs.

GIANT'S CAUSEWAY & BUSHMILLS RAILWAY

Address: Giant's Causeway Station, Runkerry Road, Bushmills, Co. Antrim, Northern Ireland   BT57 8SZ
Telephone Nº: (028) 2073-2844
Year Formed: 2002
Location: Between the distillery village of Bushmills and the Giant's Causeway

Nº of Steam Locos: 2 (not in use now)
Nº of Other Locos: 2
Nº of Members: None
Approx Nº of Visitors P.A.: 50,000
Gauge: 3 feet
Length of Line: 2 miles

GENERAL INFORMATION

Nearest Northern Ireland Railway Station: Coleraine/Portrush
Nearest Bus Station: Coleraine/Portrush
Car Parking: Car Park fee at Giant's Causeway Station is refunded upon ticket purchase. By parking at the Bushmills Station and taking the railway expensive parking charges at the Causeway itself can be avoided.
Coach Parking: Available on site
Souvenir Shop(s): Yes
Food & Drinks: At Giant's Causeway Station only

SPECIAL INFORMATION

The railway links the distillery village of Bushmills (open to visitors) to the World Heritage Site of the Giant's Causeway. The railway itself is built on the final two miles of the pioneering hydro-electric tramway which linked the Giant's Causeway to the main railway at Portrush from 1883 to 1949.

OPERATING INFORMATION

Opening Times: Daily in July and August, over St. Patrick's Day weekend and for Easter week. Also open at weekends from Easter to the end of June and in October & September. Trains run from 11.00am.
Steam Working: Please contact the railway for further information.
Prices: Adult Return £8.00   Child Return £6.00
                Concession Return £7.00
                Family Return £27.00 (2 adult + 3 child)
Note: Group rates are also available.

Detailed Directions by Car:
From Belfast take the M2 to the junction with the A26 (for Antrim, Ballymena and Coleraine). Follow the A26/M2/A26. From Ballymoney onwards Bushmills and the Giant's Causeway are well signposted. The railway is also well signposted in the immediate vicinity.

GOLDEN VALLEY LIGHT RAILWAY

Address: Butterley Station, Ripley, Derbyshire   DE5 3QZ
Telephone Nº: (01773) 747674
Year Formed: 1987
Location: Butterley to Newland Inn
Length of Line: Four-fifths of a mile

Nº of Steam Locos: 2
Nº of Other Locos: 19
Approx Nº of Visitors P.A.: 10,000
Gauge: 2 feet
Website: www.gvlr.org.uk

GENERAL INFORMATION

Nearest Mainline Station: Alfreton (6 miles)
Nearest Bus Station: Bus stop outside the Station
Car Parking: Free parking at site – ample space
Coach Parking: Free parking at site
Souvenir Shop(s): Yes – at Butterley and Swanwick
Food & Drinks: Yes – both sites

SPECIAL INFORMATION

The Golden Valley Light Railway is part of the Midland Railway – Butterley and runs from the museum site through the country park to Newlands Inn Station close to the Cromford Canal and the pub of the same name.

OPERATING INFORMATION

Opening Times: 2024 dates: Weekends, Bank Holidays and most School Holidays from 30th March to 3rd November (when the standard gauge line is operating).
Steam Working: Usually 1 weekend each month.
Prices: Adult £3.00
         Children £1.50   (Under-5s free)
         Family £7.50
         Dogs 50p (at the guard's discretion)

Detailed Directions by Car:
From All Parts: From the M1 exit at Junction 28 and take the A38 towards Derby. The railway is signposted at the junction with the B6179.

GREAT LAXEY MINE RAILWAY

Address: Laxey Valley Gardens, Laxey,
Isle of Man, IM4 6NH
Telephone Nº: (07624) 460763
Year Formed: 2004
Location of Line: Laxey Valley Gardens
Length of Line: 550 yards

Nº of Steam Locos: 2
Nº of Other Locos: 1
Approx Nº of Visitors P.A.: 7,000
Gauge: 19 inches
Website: www.laxeyminerailway.im

GENERAL INFORMATION

Nearest Mainline Station: Laxey, Manx Electric
Railway
Nearest Bus Station: Laxey
Car Parking: Available nearby
Coach Parking: Available nearby
Souvenir Shop(s): Yes
Food & Drinks: There are a number of Cafes
nearby

SPECIAL INFORMATION

The Great Laxey Mine Railway is the recently
restored surface section of the former mine
tramway, the first section of which was opened in
1823. Originally worked by ponies, these were
replaced by two steam locomotives in 1877. These
engines were scrapped in 1935 but the restored line
now uses two working replicas. A few minutes walk
from the terminus of the railway is the Lady Isabella
water wheel, the largest in the world. The railway
itself is operated entirely by volunteers.

OPERATING INFORMATION

Opening Times: 2024 dates: Every Saturday from
30th March until 28th September. A number of
Special Event Days are operated throughout the
season, details of which are advertised on the
railway's web site.
Trains run from 11.00am to 4.30pm.
Steam Working: All trains are steam-hauled
Prices: £3.00 per person (Under-3s ride free)

Detailed Directions by Car:
Laxey is situated approximately 8 miles to the north east of Douglas on the A2 coast road.

GROUDLE GLEN RAILWAY

Address: Groudle Glen, Onchan,
Isle of Man
Telephone Nº: (01624) 670453 (weekends)
Year Formed: 1982 **Re-Opened:** 1986
Location of Line: Groudle Glen
Length of Line: ¾ mile
Gauge: 2 feet

Nº of Steam Locos: 3
Nº of Other Locos: 3
Approx Nº of Visitors P.A.: 10,000
Correspondence: 29 Hawarden Avenue,
Douglas, Isle of Man IM1 4BP
Website: www.ggr.org.uk

GENERAL INFORMATION

Nearest Mainline Station: Manx Electric Railway
Nearest Bus Station: Douglas Bus Station
Car Parking: At the entrance to the Glen
Coach Parking: At the entrance to the Glen
Souvenir Shop(s): Yes
Food & Drinks: Coffee and Tea available

SPECIAL INFORMATION

The Railway runs through a picturesque glen to a
coastal headland where there are the remains of a
Victorian Zoo. The Railway was built in 1896 and
closed in 1962.

OPERATING INFORMATION

Opening Times: 2024 dates: Easter Sunday and
Monday then Sundays from 5th May to 27th
October, 11.00am to 4.30pm. Also open at other
times for special events.
Santa trains operate on 14th, 15th, 21st, 22nd and
26th December, 10.00am to 3.00pm.
Please check the web site for details of Special Events.
Steam Working: Contact the Railway for details.
Prices: Adult Return £8.00
      Child Return £4.00
      Dogs 50p
Note: Joint fares are also available to include a
Manx Electric Railway journey from Derby Castle.

Detailed Directions by Car:
The Railway is situated on the coast road to the north of Douglas.

HAMPTON & KEMPTON WATERWORKS RAILWAY

Address: Kempton Park Waterworks, Snakey Lane, Hanworth   TW13 6XH
Telephone N°: (01932) 765328
Year Formed: 2013
Web: www.hamptonkemptonrailway.org.uk
E-mail: admin@hamptonkemptonrailway.org.uk

Location: Adjacent to the Kempton Steam Museum (SatNav TW13 7ND)
Length of Line: 315 yards at present
N° of Steam Locos: 1   **Other Locos:** 3
Approx N° of Visitors P.A.: 9,600
Gauge: 2 feet

GENERAL INFORMATION

Nearest Mainline Station: Kempton Park (¾ mile)
Nearest Bus Stop: Nailhead Road Roundabout (Bus service 290)
Car Parking: Available on site
Coach Parking: Available by arrangement
Souvenir Shop(s): In the Ticket Office
Food & Drinks: Available in the Kempton Great Engine House across the road.

SPECIAL INFORMATION

The line is located on the site of the Metropolitan Water Board's industrial railway which was first opened in 1915. Work has commenced on an extension of the line to Hampton.

OPERATING INFORMATION

Opening Times: 2024 dates: Every Sunday from March to October, open from 10.30am to 4.00pm. Special Event days are scheduled each month (see the web site for full details) including Santa Specials in December. Please note that pre-booking is necessary for Special Event days.
Steam Working: All operating days when possible.
Prices: Adults £4.50
          Children £2.50 (Under-3s free)

Detailed Directions by Car:
Near the North (London) end of the M3, the A316 is elevated. Look for the two chimneys of the Kempton Steam Museum. Exit the elevated section of the A316 (Country Way) down to the roundabout below the A316 and follow the brown tourist signs for the Kempton Steam Museum, with a garage on the right and the Müller Dairy on the left, turn left into Snakey Lane and left again into Kempton Waterworks Driveway. (SATNAV: TW13 7ND)

HASTINGS MINIATURE RAILWAY

Address: Rock-a-Nore Station, Old Town, Hastings   TN34 3DW
Telephone Nº: 07789-725438
Year Formed: 1948
Location: Between Hastings Old Town and the Historic Fishing Beach & Museum
Length of Line: 680 yards

Nº of Steam Locos: 4
Nº of Other Locos: 4
Approx Nº of Visitors P.A.: 20,000
Gauge: 10¼ inches

GENERAL INFORMATION

Nearest Mainline Station: Hastings (1 mile)
Car Parking: Limited parking available nearby
Coach Parking: None
Food & Drinks: Available nearby

SPECIAL INFORMATION

The Hastings Miniature Railway, which opened on 5th June 1948, runs along the sea front area of Hastings Old Town and is a popular attraction.

OPERATING INFORMATION

Opening Times: Weekends throughout the year from 11.00am to 5.00pm (12.00pm to 4.00pm during the winter months) and also daily from May to October as well as Santa Specials in December.
Steam Working: Most days during the Summer and also for Santa Specials in December.
Prices: All Ages Return £4.00
                   All Ages Day Rover £6.00
Five tickets can be purchased for the price of four.

Detailed Directions by Car:
The Railway is located to the eastern (Fisherman's End) of Hastings Old Town, just off the A259 and next to the Hastings Fishing Museum.

Hayling Railway

Address: Eastoke Station, Sea Front Road,
Hayling Island   PO11 9HL
Telephone Nº: 07902 446340
Year Formed: 2001
Location: Eastoke to Beachlands
Length of Line: 1 mile

Nº of Steam Locos: Visiting locos only
Nº of Other Locos: 4
Approx Nº of Visitors P.A.: 25,000
Gauge: 2 feet
Website: www.haylingrailway.wixsite.com

GENERAL INFORMATION

Nearest Mainline Station: Havant
Nearest Bus Station: Beachlands
Car Parking: Spaces are available at both
Beachlands and Eastoke Corner.
Coach Parking: Beachlands and Eastoke Corner
Souvenir Shop(s): Yes, at Eastoke
Food & Drinks: Available

SPECIAL INFORMATION

The Railway runs along Hayling Island beach front
where there are fantastic views across the Solent to
the Isle of Wight.

OPERATING INFORMATION

Opening Times: Every Saturday, Sunday and
Wednesday throughout the year and daily during the
local School holidays. Various specials run at other
times of the year – please check the web site or
phone the Railway for further details.
The first train normally departs at 10.40am from
Eastoke and 11.00am from Beachlands.
Steam Working: Visiting locos only.
Please contact the railway for further information.
Prices: Adult Return £5.00
            Child Return £3.00 (Under-3s ride free)
            Senior Citizen Return £4.00
            Family Return £12.00
                 (2 adults + 2 children)

Detailed Directions by Car:
Exit the A27 at Havant Roundabout and proceed along the A3023 towards Hayling Island seafront, following
signs to Beachlands. Turn left at the funfair roundabout and follow the sefront road for 1 mile. Parking is available
behind the Eastoke Station.

HEATHERSLAW LIGHT RAILWAY

Address: Ford Forge, Heatherslaw, Cornhill-on-Tweed   TD12 4TJ
Telephone Nº: (01890) 820244
Year Formed: 1989
Location of Line: Ford & Etal Estates between Wooler & Berwick
Length of Line: 2 miles

Nº of Steam Locos: 2
Nº of Other Locos: 2
Approx Nº of Visitors P.A.: 30,000
Gauge: 15 inches
Website: www.heatherslawlightrailway.co.uk
E-mail: info@heatherslawlightrailway.co.uk

GENERAL INFORMATION

Nearest Mainline Station: Berwick-upon-Tweed (10 miles)
Nearest Bus Station: Berwick-upon-Tweed (10 mls)
Car Parking: Available on site
Coach Parking: Available on site
Souvenir Shop(s): Yes
Food & Drinks: Available

SPECIAL INFORMATION

The railway runs from Heatherslaw to Etal Castle along the banks of the River Till. A choice of semi-open and fully enclosed coaches are available to passengers, even on the wettest of days!

OPERATING INFORMATION

Opening Times: 2024 dates: Daily from 28th March to the 3rd November inclusive and also Santa Specials on 7th, 8th, 14th & 15th December. Trains run hourly from 11.00am to 3.00pm (and until 4.00pm in July & August)
Steam Working: Daily except when maintenance is being carried out on the engine.
Prices: Adult Return £9.50
        Child Return £5.50   (Ages 2-5)
        Concession Return £5.50
        Family Returns £21.00 to £26.00

Detailed Directions by Car:
From the North: Take the A697 from Coldstream and the railway is about 5 miles along.
From the South: Take the A697 from Wooler and Millfield.

HOLLYCOMBE – STEAM IN THE COUNTRY

Address: Iron Hill, Midhurst Road, Liphook, Hants. GU30 7LP
Telephone Nº: (01428) 724900
Year Formed: 1971
Location of Line: Hollycombe, Liphook
Length of Line: 1¾ miles (Narrow gauge), ¼ mile (Standard gauge) and 1,400 yards (7¼ inch gauge)

Nº of Steam Locos: 6
Nº of Other Locos: 2
Approx Nº of Visitors P.A.: 25,000
Gauge: 2 feet, Standard and 7¼ inches
Website: www.hollycombe.co.uk
E-mail: info@hollycombe.co.uk

GENERAL INFORMATION

Nearest Mainline Station: Liphook (1 mile)
Nearest Bus Station: Liphook
Car Parking: Extensive grass area
Coach Parking: Hardstanding
Souvenir Shop(s): Yes
Food & Drinks: Yes – Cafe

SPECIAL INFORMATION

The narrow gauge railway ascends to spectacular views of the Downs and is part of an extensive working steam museum.

OPERATING INFORMATION

Opening Times: 2024 dates: Sundays and Bank Holidays from 5th May to 20th October. Also open most days in August.
Steam Working: Please contact the museum for further information.
Prices: Adult £25.00
Child £20.00 (under 3s free)
Family £80.00 (2 adults + 2 children)
The prices shown are for unlimited rides on the day.

Detailed Directions by Car:
Take the A3 to Liphook and follow the brown tourist signs for the museum.

ISLE OF MAN STEAM RAILWAY

Address: Isle of Man Railways, Banks
Circus, Douglas, Isle of Man   IM1 5PT
Telephone N°: (01624) 662525
Year Formed: 1873
Location of Line: Douglas to Port Erin
Length of Line: 15½ miles

N° of Steam Locos: 16 (4 in service)
N° of Other Locos: 2
Approx N° of Visitors P.A.: 140,000
Gauge: 3 feet
Website: www.rail.im

GENERAL INFORMATION

Nearest Mainline Station: Not applicable
Car Parking: Limited parking at all stations
Coach Parking: Available at Port Erin
Souvenir Shop(s): Souvenirs are available from all
manned stations and from the shop at Port Erin
Railway Museum
Food & Drinks: Yes – Douglas & Port Erin stations

SPECIAL INFORMATION

The Isle of Man Steam Railway is operated by the
Isle of Man Government. A number of special
events are held at the railway throughout the year.

OPERATING INFORMATION

Opening Times: 2024 dates: Most days from 29th
March to 27th October but closed on Tuesdays and
Wednesdays in April and October. Also closed on
Tuesdays in May. Evening services operate during
some of the summer months. Please contact the
railway or check the web site for full details.
Steam Working: All scheduled services
Prices: Adult All-day Travel £19.00
        Child All-day Travel £9.50
        Family All-day Travel £42.00
Lower prices are charged for shorter journeys.

Detailed Directions:
By Sea from Heysham (Lancashire) or Liverpool to reach Isle of Man. By Air from Belfast, Birmingham, Dublin,
Glasgow, Gloucester, Jersey, Liverpool, Manchester, Newcastle, Bristol and London. Douglas Station is ½ mile
inland from the Sea Terminal at the end of North Quay.

KIRKLEES LIGHT RAILWAY

Address: Whistlestop Valley, Park Mill Way, Clayton West, HD8 9XJ	**No of Steam Locos:** 6
Telephone No: (01484) 865727	**No of Other Locos:** 2
Year Formed: 1991	**Approx No of Visitors P.A.:** 57,000
Location of Line: Clayton West to Shelley	**Gauge:** 15 inches
Length of Line: 3½ miles	**Website:** www.whistlestopvalley.co.uk/klr
	E-mail: info@whistlestopvalley.co.uk/klr

GENERAL INFORMATION

Nearest Mainline Station: Denby Dale (4 miles)
Nearest Bus Station: Bus stops at the bottom of Park Mill Way. Take the 435 and 436 from Wakefield or the 80 and 81 from Huddersfield.
Car Parking: Ample free parking at site
Coach Parking: Ample free parking at site
Souvenir Shop(s): Yes
Food & Drinks: Yes

SPECIAL INFORMATION

The Railway is located within the Whistlestop Valley Family Adventure Park and entry prices generally include all train rides

OPERATING INFORMATION

Opening Times: 2024 dates: Every weekend and Bank Holiday from 10th February to the 29th September and daily during school holidays from 20th July to 1st September.
Steam Working: All trains are steam-hauled (subject to availability). Train timetables vary, so please check the website for further information.
Prices: Adults £13.95 to £17.95
Children (2-16 years) £13.95 to £17.95
Concessions £10.75 to £13.45
Family Tickets £52.95 to £67.50
Note: Prices may vary on Special Event days.

Detailed Directions by Car:
The Railway is located on the A636 Wakefield to Denby Dale road. Turn off the M1 at Junction 39 and follow the A636 signposted for Denby Dale. Continue for approximately 4 miles then the railway is on the left after passing under the railway bridge and is situated at the top of the Industrial Estate, just before the village of Scissett.

LANCASHIRE MINING MUSEUM

Address: Higher Green Lane, Astley, Manchester M29 7JB	**Nº of Steam Locos:** None
Telephone Nº: (01942) 895841	**Nº of Other Locos:** 28
Year Formed: 1983	**Approx Nº of Visitors P.A.:** 6,000
Location of Line: Astley Green Colliery	**Gauge:** 2 feet
Length of Line: 440 yards	**Website:** lancashireminingmuseum.org
	E-mail: info@astleycolliery.org

GENERAL INFORMATION

Nearest Mainline Station: Salford (3 miles)
Nearest Bus Station: Leigh (3 miles)
Car Parking: Available on site
Coach Parking: Available
Food & Drinks: Snack and hot drinks available. when the Museum is open.

SPECIAL INFORMATION

The Lancashire Mining Museum houses the largest collection of underground colliery locos in the UK. The 440 yard line is used for freight demonstrations.

OPERATING INFORMATION

Opening Times: Tuesday, Thursday and weekends throughout the year except for Christmas Day and Boxing Day. The railway operates on the last Sunday of every month plus Bank Holidays. Open from 1.00pm to 4.00pm.
Steam Working: None
Prices: No admission charge to the Museum but donations are gratefully accepted.
Note: All rides cost £3.00

Detailed Directions by Car:
From All Parts: Exit the M6 at Junction 23 and take the A580 towards Manchester. After about 6 miles cross the Bridgewater Canal then take the next right signposted Higher Green. After approximately ¼ mile turn left into the Colliery grounds.

LAPPA VALLEY STEAM RAILWAY

Address: St. Newlyn East, Newquay, Cornwall   TR8 5LX
Telephone Nº: (01872) 510317
Year Formed: 1974
Location of Line: Benny Halt to East Wheal Rose, near St. Newlyn East
Length of Line: 1¼ miles

Nº of Steam Locos: 4
Nº of Other Locos: 5
Approx Nº of Visitors P.A.: 70,000
Gauge: 15 inches
Website: www.lappavalley.co.uk
E-mail: info@lappavalley.co.uk

GENERAL INFORMATION

Nearest Mainline Station: Newquay (5 miles)
Nearest Bus Station: Newquay (5 miles)
Car Parking: Free parking at Benny Halt
Coach Parking: Free parking is available at Benny Halt
Souvenir Shop(s): Yes
Food & Drinks: Yes

SPECIAL INFORMATION

The railway runs on part of the former Newquay to Chacewater branch line. Site also has a Grade II listed mine building, boating, play areas for children and 2 other miniature train rides.

OPERATING INFORMATION

Opening Times: 2024 dates: Daily from 27th March to 27th October. Also Thursdays to Sundays in November, December, part of January & February.
Steam Working: 10.40am to 4.00pm during the summer months.
Prices: Adult £17.00
       Child £15.00
       Family £59.50
          (2 adults + 2 children)
       Family £66.50
          (2 adults + 3 children)
       Concession £15.00
Note: Lower prices apply during the Winter months when services are diesel only, except for Santa Trains in December.

Detailed Directions by Car:
The railway is signposted from the A30 at the Summercourt-Mitchell bypass, from the A3075 south of Newquay and the A3058 east of Newquay.

LAUNCESTON STEAM RAILWAY

Address: The Old Gasworks, St. Thomas Road, Launceston, Cornwall   PL15 8DA
Telephone Nº: (01566) 775665
Year Formed: Opened in 1983
Location of Line: Launceston to Newmills
Length of Line: 2½ miles

Nº of Steam Locos: 4
Nº of Other Locos: 3
Gauge: 1 foot 11 ⅝ inches
Website: www.launcestonsr.co.uk

GENERAL INFORMATION

Nearest Mainline Station: Liskeard (15 miles)
Nearest Bus Station: Launceston (½ mile)
Car Parking: At the Station, Newport Industrial Estate, Launceston
Coach Parking: As above
Souvenir Shop(s): Yes – also with a bookshop
Food & Drinks: Cafe serving hot and cold meals

SPECIAL INFORMATION

The Launceston Steam Railway runs for two and a half miles through the glorious Kensey Valley along the trackbed of the old North Cornwall Railway, where once express trains from Waterloo passed.

OPERATING INFORMATION

Opening Times: 2024 dates: Opening on 26th May and then most Sundays to Tuesdays with some other days to be added to the website when known. These these may be added or cancelled at short notice, so please check the railway's website before travelling.
Steam Working: Hourly from 11.00am to 4.00pm.
Prices: Adult Return £13.50
Child Return £9.00
Family Return £37.00 (2 adult + 4 child)
Concession Return £11.50
Group rates are available upon application and prices may be subject to change.

Detailed Directions by Car:
From the East/West: Drive to Launceston via the A30 and look for the brown Steam Engine Tourist signs. Use the L.S.R. car park at the Newport Industrial Estate; From Bude/Holsworthy: Take the A388 to Launceston and follow signs for the town centre. After the river bridge turn left at the traffic lights into Newport Industrial Estate and use the L.S.R. car park. Sat Navs use the following post code: PL15 8EX.

LEADHILLS & WANLOCKHEAD RAILWAY

Address: The Station, Station Road, Leadhills,   ML12 6XS
Telephone Nº: None
Year Formed: 1983
Location of Line: Leadhills, Lanarkshire
Length of Line: ¾ mile (at present)

Nº of Steam Locos: 1 + a visiting loco
Nº of Other Locos: 6
Approx Nº of Visitors P.A.: 3,000
Gauge: 2 feet
Website: www.leadhillsrailway.co.uk

GENERAL INFORMATION

Nearest Mainline Station: Sanquhar
Nearest Bus Station: Lanark and Sanquhar
Car Parking: Available on site
Coach Parking: Available on site
Souvenir Shop(s): Yes
Food & Drinks: Yes

SPECIAL INFORMATION

Leadhills & Wanlockhead Railway is the highest adhesion railway in the UK with the summit 1,498 feet above sea level.

OPERATING INFORMATION

Opening Times: Weekends from Easter until the end of September. There are also a number of 'Special Events' during the year. Please contact the railway for further information about these. Trains run from 10.45am to 4.00pm on operating days.
Steam Working: Please check the website for details.
Prices: Adult Return £7.50
　　　　　Child Return £3.50
　　　　　Concession Return £6.00
　　　　　Family Return £18.00
　　　　　　　(2 adults and up to 2 children)

Detailed Directions by Car:
From the South: Exit the M74 at Junction 14 and follow the A702 to Elvanfoot. Turn right onto the B7040 and follow to Leadhills. Turn left at the T-junction and Station Road is a short distance on the left; From the North: Exit the M74 at Junction 13 for Abington and follow signs for Leadhills along the B797. Station Road is on the left shortly after entering Leadhills.

LEIGHTON BUZZARD RAILWAY

Address: Pages Park Station, Billington Road, Leighton Buzzard, Beds. LU7 4TN
Telephone Nº: (01525) 373888
Year Formed: 1967
Location of Line: Leighton Buzzard
Length of Line: 3 miles

Nº of Steam Locos: 8
Nº of Other Locos: 55
Approx Nº of Visitors P.A.: 20,000
Gauge: 2 feet
Website: www.buzzrail.co.uk

GENERAL INFORMATION

Nearest Mainline Station: Leighton Buzzard (2 miles)
Nearest Bus Station: Leighton Buzzard (¾ mile)
Car Parking: Free parking adjacent
Coach Parking: Free parking adjacent
Souvenir Shop(s): Yes
Food & Drinks: Yes

SPECIAL INFORMATION

The railway was constructed in 1919 to carry sand from local quarries using surplus materials from World War I battlefield supply lines. Now a working museum, it transports passengers and is operated by volunteers.

OPERATING INFORMATION

Opening Times: 2024 dates: Sundays from 10th March to 27th October plus Bank Holiday weekends. Also open on some Saturdays and weekdays. Trains run from 10.30am to 4.00pm and a return journey takes 80 minutes. Christmas and New Year services operate on some dates in December.
Please visit the railway's web site for further details.
Steam Working: Most operating days.
Prices: Adult £11.80
Child £8.15 (Under-2s ride for free)
Concession £10.40
Note: The prices shown above do not include an optional Gift Aid donation.

Detailed Directions by Car:
Travel to Leighton Buzzard then follow the brown tourist signs showing a steam train. Pages Park Station is situated ¾ mile to the south of the Town Centre. From the A505/A4146 bypass, turn towards Leighton Buzzard at the roundabout following the 'Narrow Gauge Railway' brown tourist signs.

LINCOLNSHIRE COAST LIGHT RAILWAY

Address: Skegness Water Leisure Park, Walls Lane, Ingoldmells PE25 1JF	**Nº of Steam Locos:** 1
Telephone Nº: (01754) 899400(option 1)	**Nº of Other Locos:** 8
Year Formed: 1960 (re-opened in 2009)	**Approx Nº of Visitors P.A.:** 5,000
Location of Line: Skegness	**Gauge:** 2 feet
Length of Line: ¾ miles	**Website:** www.lclr.co.uk
	E-mail: john@chappellandcosurveyors.co.uk

GENERAL INFORMATION

Nearest Mainline Station: Skegness (3 miles)
Nearest Bus Station: Butlins (½ miles)
Car Parking: Free parking available on site
Coach Parking: Free parking available on site
Souvenir Shop(s): None
Food & Drinks: Available

SPECIAL INFORMATION

The railway re-opened in 2009, after relocating from its' original home in Humberston, where it ran from 1960 to 1985. It is home to a unique collection of English narrow gauge railway carriages, vehicles and locomotives, many of which saw service in the trench warfare during the First World War.

OPERATING INFORMATION

Opening Times: 2024 dates: 20th & 21st April; 4th, 5th, 11th, 12th, 18th, 19th & 26th May; 15th June; 20th & 27th July; 3rd, 5th, 7th, 10th, 12th, 14th, 17th, 19th, 21st, 24th, 26th, 28th and 31st August; 2nd September and 26th October. Further dates may be added to the timetable during the year. Please check the web site for details. Trains run between 10.30am and 3.40pm.
Steam Working: Please check web site for details
Prices: Adults £2.00
    Children £2.00 (Under-3s ride free)
    Family Tickets £5.00

Detailed Directions by Car:
From All Parts: Take the A52 North from Skegness (signposted for Ingoldmells) and continue for 3 miles. Turn left onto Walls Lane opposite the Butlins signposted for the Water Leisure Park. After ¼ mile turn left into the Park and follow the signs for the Railway.

LITTLEHAMPTON RAILWAY

Address: Mewsbrook Park, Hendon Avenue, Littlehampton BN16 2LX	**N° of Steam Locos:** None
Telephone N°: 07436 562933	**N° of Other Locos:** 3
Information N°: 07746 907817	**Approx N° of Visitors P.A.:** 18,000
Year Formed: 1948	**Gauge:** 12¼ inches
Location of Line: Mewsbrook Park	**Website:** www.littlehamptonminiaturerailway.com
Length of Line: ½ mile	**E-mail:** info@littlehamptonminiaturerailway.com

GENERAL INFORMATION

Nearest Mainline Station: Littlehampton (1 mile)
Nearest Bus Station: Littlehampton
Car Parking: Available at the swimming pool, at East Green and along the Sea Wall.
Coach Parking: Available at the swimming pool
Souvenir Shop(s): During special event days only
Food & Drinks: Cafes are adjacent to both stations

SPECIAL INFORMATION

The Littlehampton Railway is the oldest 12¼ inch gauge railway in the UK and runs from Mewsbrook Park to Norfolk Gardens. The railway is surrounded by a variety of leisure attractions including a boating lake and a 9-hole golf course.

OPERATING INFORMATION

Opening Times: 2024 dates: Weekends and School Holidays from 29th March to 3rd November (weather permitting). Trains run daily from 11.00am then every 30 minutes until 4.00pm. Santa Specials also operate on 14th and 15th December.
Steam Working: None at present
Prices: Adult Return £3.00
   Child Return £2.00 (Under-3s ride free)
   Family Ticket Return £9.00
   (2 adults + 2 children)

Detailed Directions by Car:
From All Parts: Take the A27 Brighton to Portsmouth road and follow signs for Littlehampton. Upon entering Littlehampton, follow signs for the Swimming Pool/Sea Front and, when you reach the Beach Road (which runs along parallel to the sea), head east and park either at East Green or further along to the Swimming Pool.

LLANBERIS LAKE RAILWAY

Address: Gilfach Ddu, Padarn Country Park, Llanberis, Gwynedd LL55 4TY
Telephone Nº: (01286) 870549
Year Formed: 1970
Location of Line: Just off the A4086 Caernarfon to Capel Curig road at Llanberis
Length of Line: 2½ miles

Nº of Steam Locos: 3
Nº of Other Locos: 2
Approx Nº of Visitors P.A.: 80,000
Gauge: 1 foot 11½ inches
Website: www.lake-railway.co.uk
E-mail: sales@lake-railway.co.uk

GENERAL INFORMATION

Nearest Mainline Station: Bangor (8 miles)
Nearest Bus Station: Caernarfon (6 miles) (there is a bus stop by Llanberis Station)
Car Parking: £4.00 Council car park on site
Coach Parking: Ample free parking on site
Souvenir Shop(s): Yes
Food & Drinks: Yes

SPECIAL INFORMATION

Llanberis Lake Railway runs along part of the trackbed of the Padarn Railway which transported slates for export and closed in 1961.
Note: The Welsh Slate Museum is situated adjacent to the Railway.

OPERATING INFORMATION

Opening Times: 2024 dates: Open most days from 17th March to 3rd November excluding some Saturdays in April, May and September and some Fridays and Saturdays in October. Open Tuesdays to Thursdays only in November and on some dates in December. Please check out the railway's web site where an online booking feature is also available.
Steam Working: Every operating day.
Trains generally run from 11.00am to 4.00pm.
Prices: Adult £10.50
Child £6.00
Concessions £9.50
Family tickets £15.00 to £60.00
(depending on the numbers in the family)

Detailed Directions by Car:
The railway is situated just off the A4086 Caernarfon to Capel Curig road. Follow signs for Padarn Country Park.

LYNTON & BARNSTAPLE RAILWAY

Address: Woody Bay Station, Martinhoe Cross, Parracombe, Devon EX31 4RA	**Nº of Steam Locos:** 2
Telephone Nº: (01598) 763487	**Nº of Other Locos:** 3
Year Formed: 1993	**Approx Nº of Visitors P.A.:** 50,000
Location of Line: North Devon	**Gauge:** 1 foot 11½ inches
Length of Line: One mile	**Website:** www.lynton-rail.co.uk
	E-mail: enquiries@lynton-rail.co.uk

GENERAL INFORMATION

Nearest Mainline Station: Barnstaple
Nearest Bus Station: Barnstaple
Car Parking: Available at Woody Bay Station
Coach Parking: Available by prior arrangement
Souvenir Shop(s): Yes – at Woody Bay Station
Food & Drinks: Available at Woody Bay Station

SPECIAL INFORMATION

Original Lynton & Barnstaple Railway carriages built in 1898 and 1903 are now operating a regular passenger service. At present, trains are only running between Woody Bay Station and Killington Lane Halt due to reconstruction work.

OPERATING INFORMATION

Opening Times: 2024 dates: Open most days from 29th March to 3rd November with the exception of some Fridays. Please check with the railway for exact dates.
Steam Working: All trains are steam-hauled except in the event of breakdown.
Prices: Adult Return £9.00
Students Return (ages 14-18) £7.00
Under-14s ride free of charge
Family Ticket £30.00
(2 Adults + 3 Children)
Note: Upgrades to First Class are £3.50 per person.

Detailed Directions by Car:
From All Parts: Woody Bay Station is located alongside the A39 halfway between Lynton and Blackmoor Gate and one mile north-east of the village of Parracombe.

MANX ELECTRIC RAILWAY

Address: Manx Electric Railway, Banks Circus, Douglas, Isle of Man IM1 5PT
Telephone Nº: (01624) 662525
Year Formed: 1873
Location of Line: Douglas to Ramsey
Length of Line: 17½ miles

Nº of Steam Locos: None
Nº of Other Locos: over 20 vintage units
Approx Nº of Visitors P.A.: 140,000
Gauge: 3 feet
Website: www.rail.im

GENERAL INFORMATION

Nearest Mainline Station: Not applicable
Car Parking: Limited parking at all stations
Coach Parking: Available at Port Erin
Souvenir Shop(s): Souvenirs are available from all manned stations and from the shop at Port Erin Railway Museum.
Food & Drinks: Yes – Douglas & Port Erin stations

SPECIAL INFORMATION

The Isle of Man Steam Railway is operated by the Isle of Man Government. A number of special events are held at the railway throughout the year.

OPERATING INFORMATION

Opening Times: 2024 dates: Most days from 29th March to 27th October but closed on Tuesdays and Wednesdays in April and October. Also closed on Tuesdays in May. Evening services operate during some of the summer months. Please contact the railway or check the web site for full details.
Steam Working: All scheduled services
Prices: Adult All-day Travel £19.00
Child All-day Travel £9.50
Family All-day Travel £42.00
Note: Lower prices are available for other journeys.

Detailed Directions:
By Sea from Heysham (Lancashire) or Liverpool to reach the Isle of Man. By Air from Belfast, Birmingham, Dublin, Glasgow, Gloucester, Jersey, Liverpool, Manchester, Newcastle, Bristol and London. Douglas Station is situated ½ mile inland from the Sea Terminal at the end of North Quay.

MARGAM PARK RAILWAY

Address: Margam Country Park, Port Talbot SA13 2TJ	**Nº of Steam Locos:** None
Telephone Nº: (01639) 881635	**Nº of Other Locos:** 1
Year Formed: 1976	**Approx Nº of Visitors P.A.:** 200,000 (to the Park itself, not just the railway!)
Location of Line: Margam Country Park	**Gauge:** 2 feet
Length of Line: Almost 1½ miles	**Website:** www.margamcountrypark.co.uk

GENERAL INFORMATION

Nearest Mainline Station: Port Talbot (3 miles)
Nearest Bus Station: Port Talbot (3 miles)
Car Parking: Available on site for a £6.00 charge
Coach Parking: Available
Souvenir Shop(s): Yes
Food & Drinks: Available

SPECIAL INFORMATION

Set in 1,000 acres of glorious parkland, Margam Country Park features an 18th Century Orangery, a Tudor-Gothic Victorian Mansion House and a 12th Century Chapter House.

OPERATING INFORMATION

Opening Times: 2024 dates: The railway operates on weekends, Bank Holidays and daily throughout the school holidays during the spring and summer seasons. The railway is closed during the autumn and winter months.
Please check the website for further information.
Steam Working: None at present
Prices: Adults £3.00
Children £1.65 (Under-3s ride for free)
Concessions £1.65
Above prices are for single journeys.
Note: Entrance to Margam Park is usually free, but there may be admission charges on special event days (usually Bank Holidays).
Please check the website for further details.

Detailed Directions by Car:
From All Parts: Exit the M4 at Junction 38 and take the A48 towards Pyle following the brown tourist signs for Margam Country Park. The Park is situated on the left hand side of the road.

MOUNTSORREL RAILWAY MUSEUM

Address: 240 Swithland Lane, Mountsorrel, LE7 7UE	**Nº of Steam Locos:** 2 (1 in storage)
Telephone Nº: (0116) 237 4591	**Nº of Other Locos:** 1
Year Formed: 2007 (opened 2015)	**Approx Nº of Visitors P.A.:** Not known
Location: Swithland Sidings & Nunckley Hill Quarry, Mountsorrel.	**Gauge:** Standard & 2 Foot
Length: The 2 foot line is 150 yards long	**Website:** www.heritage-centre.co.uk

GENERAL INFORMATION

Nearest Mainline Station: Loughborough (1¾ mile)
Nearest Bus Station: Loughborough
Car Parking: Available on site
Coach Parking: Available on site
Food & Drinks: Granite Coffee Shop (free entry)

SPECIAL INFORMATION

The Museum occupies a location at the end of the 1¼ mile Mountsorrel Branch Line which is operated by the Great Central Railway at Loughborough. Train rides along the 2 foot line are available.

OPERATING INFORMATION

Opening Times: 2024 dates: Open daily 10.00am to 4.45pm. Please check the website for details of Special Event days.
Steam Working: None at present
Prices: Adult £2.00
Child £1.00 (Ages 2 to 15)
Note: Prices shown are for entry to both the Centre and the Museum, however there is a similar extra charge for 3 circuit rides on the 2 foot gauge railway.

Detailed Directions by Car:
Take the Southbound A6 from Loughborough and exit after 4½ miles into Granite Way. Continue into Mountsorrel, turn left at the roundabout onto Loughborough Road, then right at the second roundabout onto The Green. Continue into Rothley Road, turn right into Halstead Road and continue to the end of the road before turning right into Swithland Lane. The Heritage Centre is a short distance along on the left.

NORTH INGS FARM MUSEUM

Address: Fen Road, Dorrington, Lincoln LN4 3QB	**N° of Steam Locos:** 1
Telephone N°: (01526) 833100	**N° of Other Locos:** 8
Year Formed: 1971	**Approx N° of Visitors P.A.:** Not recorded
Location of Line: Dorrington	**Gauge:** 2 feet
Length of Line: A third of a mile	**Website:** www.northingsfarmmuseum.co.uk
	E-mail: info@northingsfarmmuseum.co.uk

GENERAL INFORMATION

Nearest Mainline Station: Ruskington (3 miles)
Nearest Bus Station: Dorrington (1 mile)
Car Parking: Free parking available on site
Coach Parking: Free parking available on site
Souvenir Shop(s): None
Food & Drinks: None

SPECIAL INFORMATION

The railway forms part of an agricultural machinery and tractor museum, originally built to serve the farm.

OPERATING INFORMATION

Opening Times: 2024 dates: The first Sunday of the month from 7th April through to 6th October inclusive. Open from 10.00am to 5.00pm
Steam Working: Subject to availability. Please contact the Farm Museum for further information.
Prices: Adult £3.00
Child £1.50

Detailed Directions by Car:
From All Parts: North Ings Farm Museum is situated just off the B1188 between Lincoln and Sleaford. Turn into Dorrington Village at the Musician's Arms public house, pass through the village and under the railway bridge. The Museum entrance is on the right after 600 yards and the Museum is then ½ mile down the farm road.

NORTH BAY MINIATURE RAILWAY

Address: Burniston Road, Scarborough, North Yorkshire   YO12 6PF
Telephone N°: (01723) 368791
Year Opened: 1931
Location: Peasholm Park to Scalby Mills
Length of Line: 1 mile

N° of Steam Locos: None
N° of Other Locos: 4
N° of Members: None
Approx N° of Visitors P.A.: 200,000
Gauge: 20 inches
Website: www.snbr.org.uk
E-mail: info@snbr.org.uk

GENERAL INFORMATION

Nearest Mainline Station: Scarborough (¾mile)
Nearest Bus Station: Scarborough
Car Parking: Adjacent to the railway
Coach Parking: Adjacent to the railway
Souvenir Shop(s): Yes
Food & Drinks: Drinks and snacks are available from the Sidings Snack Shack.

SPECIAL INFORMATION

The North Bay Miniature Railway was opened in 1931 and operates between Northstead Manor and Scalby Mills for the Sea Life Centre.

OPERATING INFORMATION

Opening Times: 2024 dates: Daily from 23rd March until 3rd November and Santa Specials run on December weekends before Christmas. Services then operate at weekends from mid-February to Easter. Please check the website for further details.
Steam Working: None
Prices: Adult Return £5.49
        Child Return £3.99 (Ages 3-15)

Detailed Directions by Car:
From All Parts: Take the A64, A165 or A170 to Scarborough and follow the signs for North Bay Leisure Park. The railway is situated just off the A165 opposite Peasholm Park. Alternatively, follow signs for the Sea Life Centre for Scalby Mills Station.

OLD KILN LIGHT RAILWAY

Address: RuralLifeLivingMuseum, Reeds Road, Tilford, Farnham, GU10 2DL	**No of Steam Locos:** 3
Telephone No: (01252) 795571	**No of Other Locos:** 8
Year Formed: 1975	**Approx No of Visitors P.A.:** 21,000
Location: 3 miles south of Farnham	**Gauge:** 2 feet
Length of Line: ¾ mile	**Website:** oldkilnlightrailway.co.uk
	E-mail: info@oldkilnlightrailway.co.uk

GENERAL INFORMATION

Nearest Mainline Station: Farnham (4 miles)
Nearest Bus Station: Farnham
Car Parking: Free parking available on site
Coach Parking: Free parking available on site
Souvenir Shop(s): Yes
Food & Drinks: Available

SPECIAL INFORMATION

The Railway is part of the Rural Life Living Museum at Tilford. The Museum contains the biggest country life collection in the South of England with a wide range of attractions. A line extension to ¾ mile has recently been opened.

OPERATING INFORMATION

Opening Times: 2024 dates: The Centre is open most weekends from 16th March to 29th September and on several other Wednesdays. Please check the web site for details.
Steam Working: During Special Events only.
Prices: Adult £11.00
Child £8.00 (Under-4s free)
Concessions £9.75
Family Ticket 30.00 to £38.00
(Depends on number in family)
Note: Prices shown are for entry to the Rural Life Centre without a Gift Aid donation but Train Rides cost an extra £3.00 per person.

Detailed Directions by Car:
The Rural Life Centre is situated 3 miles south of Farnham. From Farnham take the A287 southwards before turning left at Millbridge crossroads into Reeds Road. The Centre is on the left after about ½ mile, just after the Frensham Garden Centre; From the A3: Turn off at the Hindhead crossroads and head north to Tilford. Pass through Tilford, cross the River Wey then turn left into Reeds Road. The Centre is on the right after ½ mile.

PERRYGROVE RAILWAY

Address: Perrygrove Railway, Coleford, Gloucestershire GL16 8QB	**Nº of Steam Locos**: 5
Telephone Nº: (01594) 834991	**Nº of Other Locos**: 3
Year Formed: 1996	**Approx Nº of Visitors P.A.**: 30,000
Location of Line: ½ mile south of Coleford	**Gauge**: 15 inches
Length of Line: ¾ mile	**Website**: www.perrygrove.co.uk
	Email: info@perrygrove.co.uk

GENERAL INFORMATION

Nearest Mainline Station: Lydney (for Parkend)
Nearest Bus Station: Bus stops in Coleford
Car Parking: Free parking available on site
Coach Parking: Free parking on site
Souvenir Shop(s): Yes
Food & Drinks: Sandwiches & light refreshments are available

SPECIAL INFORMATION

Perrygrove is a unique railway with 4 stations, all with access to private woodland walks. Lots of picnic tables are available in the open and under cover. There is also an indoor village with secret passages, a play area and an exciting Treetop Adventure accessible to all.

OPERATING INFORMATION

Opening Times: Open every weekend, Tuesday and Thursday throughout the year and daily during the local school holidays. A number of Special Events are also held throughout the year including Santa Specials on weekends in December (pre-booking is essential for these). Please contact the railway for details. Opening hours vary depending on the season so please check the website for details of the times before visiting.
Steam Working: Some services are steam-hauled, depending on the time of the year and driver experience courses are also available.
Prices: Adults: £10.00 (Annual ticket £44.00)
Children: £8.50 (Annual ticket £35.50)
(Under-2s ride free)
Concessions £7.50 (Annual ticket £32.50)

Detailed Directions by Car:
From All Parts: Travel to Coleford, Gloucestershire. Upon reaching the vicinity of Coleford, the Perrygrove Railway is clearly signposted with brown tourist signs from all directions. SATNAVs use this post code: GL16 8QB

RAVENGLASS & ESKDALE RAILWAY

Address: Ravenglass, Cumbria CA18 1SW	**Gauge:** 15 inches
Telephone Nº: (01229) 717171	**Nº of Steam Locos:** 7
Year Formed: 1875	**Nº of Other Locos:** 8
Location: The Lake District National Park	**Approx Nº of Visitors P.A.:** 120,000
Length of Line: 7 miles	**Website:** www.ravenglass-railway.co.uk
	E-mail: steam@ravenglass-railway.co.uk

GENERAL INFORMATION

Nearest Mainline Station: Ravenglass (adjacent)
Nearest Bus Stop: Ravenglass
Car Parking: Available at both terminals
Coach Parking: At Ravenglass
Souvenir Shop(s): Yes   **Food & Drinks:** Yes

SPECIAL INFORMATION

The Ravenglass & Eskdale Railway is one of the oldest and longest narrow gauge railways in England, known affectionately as 'La'al Ratty', meaning "little railway" in the old Cumbrian dialect. The heritage steam engines transport passengers from Ravenglass, the only coastal village in the Lake District, through seven miles of spectacular scenery within sight of England's highest mountains, the Scafell Range, through to Dalegarth for Boot, some 210ft above sea level.

OPERATING INFORMATION

Opening Times: 2024 dates: The service runs daily from 16th March until 3rd November inclusive. Trains also run daily during February half-term and Christmas School Holidays and Santa Specials operate on weekends and other dates in December. Open from 9.00am to 5.00pm (sometimes later during high season).
Steam Working: Most services are steam-hauled.
Prices: Adult £23.00
        Child £15.50 (Ages 3 to 17)
        Under-3s travel free
        Family Tickets £46.00 to £69.00
        (depends on number in family)
Note: Prices shown are for return journeys. Director's Saloon upgrades are available and discounts are available for online ticket purchases.

Detailed Directions by Car:
The railway is situated just off the main A595 Western Lake District road.

RHYL MINIATURE RAILWAY

Address: Marine Lake, Wellington Road, Rhyl LL18 1AQ
Telephone Nº: (01352) 759109
E-mail: info@rhylminiaturerailway.co.uk
Year Formed: 1911
Location of Line: Rhyl
Length of Line: 1 mile

Nº of Steam Locos: 5
Nº of Other Locos: 3
Approx Nº of Visitors P.A.: 20,000
Gauge: 15 inches
Website: www.rhylminiaturerailway.co.uk
E-mail: info@rhylminiaturerailway.co.uk

GENERAL INFORMATION

Nearest Mainline Station: Rhyl (1 mile)
Nearest Bus Station: Rhyl (1 mile)
Car Parking: Car Park near the Railway
Coach Parking: Available nearby
Souvenir Shop(s): Yes
Food & Drinks: Available

SPECIAL INFORMATION

The trust operates the oldest Miniature Railway in the UK. The principal locomotive and train have been operating there since the 1920's.

OPERATING INFORMATION

Opening Times: 2024 dates: Every weekend from 23rd March until the 1st October. Also open on Bank Holiday Mondays and Fridays during June and July and then daily from 5th July to 1st September, with Santa Trains operating during December. Trains run from 10.30am to 4.00pm.
Steam Working: Every Sunday and also Friday to Saturday during the School Summer Holidays.
Prices: Adult £3.50
Child £2.50 (Ages 2 to 14)

Detailed Directions by Car:
From All Parts: The Railway is located behind the west end of Rhyl Promenade.

ROMNEY, HYTHE & DYMCHURCH RAILWAY

Address: New Romney Station,
New Romney, Kent   TN28 8PL
Telephone Nº: (01797) 362353
E-mail: info@rhdr.org.uk
Year Formed: 1927
Location of Line: Approximately 5 miles
west of Folkestone
Length of Line: 13½ miles

Nº of Steam Locos: 11
Nº of Other Locos: 5
Approx Nº of Visitors P.A.: 160,000
Gauge: 15 inches
Website: www.rhdr.org.uk
Email: info@rhdr.org.uk

GENERAL INFORMATION

Nearest Mainline Station: Folkestone Central
(5 miles) or Rye
Nearest Bus Station: Folkestone (then take the bus
to Hythe)
Car Parking: Free parking at all major stations
Coach Parking: At New Romney & Dungeness
Souvenir Shop(s): Yes – 4 at various stations
Food & Drinks: 2 Cafes serving food and drinks
plus a tea shop at Hythe Station.

SPECIAL INFORMATION

Opened in 1927 as 'The World's Smallest Public
Railway'. Now the only 15" gauge tourist main
line railway in the world. Double track, 7 stations.

OPERATING INFORMATION

Opening Times: 2024 dates: A daily service runs
from 29th March to 3rd November. Also open on
some weekends in February, March and November,
daily during School half-terms and for Santa
Specials during December.
Steam Working: All operational days.
Prices: Adult Day Rover £28.00
       Child Day Rover £14.00 (Ages 3-15 years)
       Concessions Day Rover £25.00
       Family Day Rover £69.00
              (2 adults + 3 children)
Note: Lower prices apply for shorter journeys.

Detailed Directions by Car:
Exit the M20 at Junction 11 then follow signs to Hythe and the brown tourist signs for the railway. Alternatively,
Take the A259 to New Romney and follow the brown tourist signs for the railway.

ROYAL VICTORIA RAILWAY

Address: Royal Victoria Country Park, Netley, Southampton SO31 5GA
Telephone N°: (023) 8045-6246
Year Formed: 1995
Location of Line: Netley
Length of Line: 1 mile

N° of Steam Locos: 7
N° of Other Locos: 4
Approx N° of Visitors P.A.: Not known
Gauge: 10¼ inches
Website: www.royalvictoriarailway.co.uk

GENERAL INFORMATION

Nearest Mainline Station: Netley
Nearest Bus Station: Southampton
Car Parking: Paid parking available on site (using a barrier system)
Coach Parking: None
Food & Drinks: Available in the Country Park

SPECIAL INFORMATION

The railway runs through the grounds of an old Victorian hospital and has good views of the Solent and the Isle of Wight. The Park covers 200 acres including woodland, grassland, beaches, picnic sites and a play area.

OPERATING INFORMATION

Opening Times: Weekends throughout the year and daily during local school holidays. Trains run from 11.00am to 4.30pm. The railway also opens by appointment for larger parties.
Steam Working: On special event days only. Please phone for further details.
Prices: Adult Return £1.75
Child Return £1.25 (Under-2s ride free)
Note: Prices may be higher on Special Event days.

Detailed Directions by Car:
From All Parts: Exit the M27 at Junction 8 and follow the Brown Tourist signs for the Royal Victoria Country Park. You will reach the Park after approximately 3 miles. Do not use Sat Nav as the directions will be incorrect!

RUISLIP LIDO RAILWAY

Address: Reservoir Road, Ruislip, Middlesex HA4 7TY	**N° of Steam Locos:** 1
Telephone N°: (01895) 622595	**N° of Other Locos:** 5
Year Formed: 1979	**Approx N° of Visitors P.A.:** 60,000
Location of Line: Trains travel from Ruislip Lido to Woody Bay	**Gauge:** 12 inches
Length of Line: 1¼ miles	**Website:** www.ruisliplidorailway.org

GENERAL INFORMATION

Nearest Mainline Station: West Ruislip (2 miles)
Nearest Bus Station: Ruislip Underground Station
Car Parking: Free parking available at the Lido
Coach Parking: Free parking available at the Lido
Souvenir Shop(s): Yes
Food & Drinks: A Cafe is open on weekends and Bank Holidays. A Pub/Restaurant is open daily.

SPECIAL INFORMATION

The steam locomotive, 'Mad Bess' used by Ruislip Lido Railway was actually built by the members over a 12 year period!

OPERATING INFORMATION

Opening Times: 2024 dates: Weekends from 10th February to 24th November. Daily from 20th July to 1st September. Also Santa Trains run in December.
Steam Working: Most weekends from May to September.
Prices: Adult Return £4.00 (Single fare £3.00)
Child Return £3.00 (Single fare £2.00)
Family Return £12.00 (Single £8.00)
(2 adults + 2 children)
Note: Under-3s travel for free

Detailed Directions by Car:
From All Parts: Follow the signs from the A40 and take the A4180 through Ruislip before turning left onto the B469.

SALTBURN MINIATURE RAILWAY

Address: Valley Gardens, Saltburn
Telephone Nº: (01287) 622712
Year Formed: 1947
Location of Line: Cat Nab Station to
Forest Halt Station, Saltburn
Website: www.saltburn-miniature-railway.org.uk
E-mail: info@saltburn-miniature-railway.org.uk

Nº of Steam Locos: 1
Nº of Other Locos: 3
Approx Nº of Visitors P.A.: 20,000
Gauge: 15 inches
Length of Line: ¾ mile

GENERAL INFORMATION

Nearest Mainline Station: Saltburn (½ mile)
Nearest Bus Station: Saltburn (½ mile)
Car Parking: Available at Cat Nab Station
Coach Parking: Glen Side (at the top of the bank)
Souvenir Shop(s): At Cat Nab Station
Food & Drinks: None

OPERATING INFORMATION

Opening Times: Weekends and Bank Holidays
from Easter until the end of September. Also open
Tuesday to Friday during the Summer School
Holidays. All services operate weather permitting.
Trains run from 1.00pm to 5.00pm.
Steam Working: Please contact the railway for
details.
Prices: Adult Return £2.00 (Adult Single £1.50)
         Child Return 1.00 (Child Single 50p)
Note: Family day tickets cost £10.00
       Under-5s ride free of charge.

Detailed Directions by Car:
Follow the A174 from Middlesbrough (West) or Whitby (East) to Saltburn-by-the-Sea. Cat Nab Station with its
adjoining car park is situated by the beach, directly off the C74 (C174).

SHERWOOD FOREST RAILWAY

Address: Gorsethorpe Lane, Edwinstowe, Mansfield NG21 9HL	**No of Steam Locos:** 2
Telephone No: (01623) 515339	**No of Other Locos:** 3
Year Formed: 1999	**Approx No of Visitors P.A.:** 5,000
Location of Line: Between Mansfield Woodhouse and Edwinstowe	**Gauge:** 15 inches
Length of Line: 680 yards	**Website:** www.sherwoodforestrailway.com
	E-mail: info@sherwoodforestrailway.com

GENERAL INFORMATION

Nearest Mainline Station: Mansfield (7 miles)
Nearest Bus Station: Mansfield (7 miles)
Car Parking: Free parking available on site
Coach Parking: Available on site
Souvenir Shop(s): Yes
Food & Drinks: Available

SPECIAL INFORMATION

The Railway runs through the grounds of Shaw-Browne Estates which has play areas for children and picnic areas. An extension to double the length of the line is planned.

OPERATING INFORMATION

Opening Times: 2024 dates: Open daily from March through to the end of November. Trains run from 11.00am to dusk on most days.
Steam Working: Every operating day.
Prices: Adults £3.00
         Chidren £2.50

Detailed Directions by Car:
From the A1: Turn off at the Worksop roundabout and head to Ollerton. Follow the A6075 through Edwinstowe and towards Mansfield Woodhouse, then turn left at the double mini-roundabout. The railway is on the right after approximately 200 yards; From Nottingham: Head to Ollerton, then as above; From the M1: Exit at Junction 27 and head into Mansfield. Follow signs to Mansfield Woodhouse and then on towards Edwinstowe. From here, follow the tourist signs for the Steam Railway.

SHIBDEN MINIATURE RAILWAY

Address: Shibden Park, Listers Lane,
Halifax HX3 6XG
Telephone Nº: 07854 658635
Year Formed: 1983
Location of Line: Halifax, West Yorkshire
Length of Line: 1 km

Nº of Steam Locos: 1 (in storage)
Nº of Other Locos: 2
Approx Nº of Visitors P.A.: Not known
Gauge: 10¼ inches
E-mail: shibdenrailway@hotmail.com

GENERAL INFORMATION

Nearest Mainline Station: Halifax (2 miles)
Nearest Bus Station: Halifax (2 miles)
Car Parking: Available on site
Coach Parking: Available
Souvenir Shop(s): None
Food & Drinks: Available in the Park

SPECIAL INFORMATION

The railway operates in the public park surrounding
Shibden Hall, a historic house which dates back to
around 1420.

OPERATING INFORMATION

Opening Times: Weekends throughout the year
from Easter to October and daily during the School
Holidays from 11.00am to 5.00pm, weather
permitting.
Steam Working: None at present
Prices: Adults £2.50
         Children £2.50

Detailed Directions by Car:
From All Parts: Exit the M62 at Junction 25 and take the A644 to Hipperholme then follow the A58 towards
Halifax. The Park is on the left of the A58 as you enter Halifax and is well-signposted.

SITTINGBOURNE & KEMSLEY LIGHT RAILWAY

Address: The Wall, Sittingbourne Retail Park, Sittingbourne, Kent ME10 2XD
Info/Talking Timetable: (01795) 424899
Contact Nº: 07973 192938
Year Formed: 1969
Location of Line: North of Sittingbourne
Length of Line: 2 miles

Nº of Steam Locos: 9 (2 Standard gauge)
Nº of Other Locos: 4
Approx Nº of Visitors P.A.: 7,000
Gauge: 2 feet 6 inches
Website: www.sklr.net
E-mail: info@sklr.net

GENERAL INFORMATION

Nearest Mainline Station: Sittingbourne (¼ mile)
Nearest Bus Station: Sittingbourne Mainline station
Car Parking: Sittingbourne Retail Park (behind KFC)
Coach Parking: Sittingbourne Retail Park
Souvenir Shop(s): Yes   **Food & Drinks:** Yes

SPECIAL INFORMATION

The railway is the only original preserved narrow gauge industrial steam railway in S.E. England (once the Bowaters Paper Company Railway). The first kilometre of the line passes over the century-old Milton Regis Viaduct before crossing Milton Creek Country Park to the operational paper mill and Kemsley Down. Other attractions include a Museum, garden railway, Children's play area & Wildlife Garden.

OPERATING INFORMATION

Opening Times: 2024 dates: Sundays and Bank Holiday weekends from 29th March to 29th September. Also open on Wednesdays in August and for Santa Specials on weekends from 2nd to 22nd December. Please visit the website for details of other Special Events held throughout the year.
Steam Working: Trains normally run from 1.00pm, but from 11.00am on Bank Holiday weekends and Sundays in August. The last train runs at 4.00pm (except for during some special events).
Prices: Adult Return £8.00
             Child Return £4.00 (Under-3s ride free)
             Senior Citizen Return £7.00
             Family Return £22.00 (2 Adult + 4 Child)
Note: Different fares may apply on special event days.

Detailed Directions by Car:
From East or West: Take the M2 (or M20) to the A249 and travel towards Sittingbourne. Exit onto the B2006 signposted for Bobbing and continue along the B2006 into the town centre. At the roundabout by the garage turn right into Mill Way (signposted for Kent Science Park) and then follow the brown heritage signs into Sittingbourne Retail Park for the railway. Free parking is available behind KFC and opposite Pizza Hut.

SNAEFELL MOUNTAIN RAILWAY

Address: Snaefell Mountain Railway, Banks Circus, Douglas, Isle of Man, IM1 5PT **Telephone Nº:** (01624) 662525 **Year Formed:** 1873 **Gauge:** 3 feet 6 inches	**Location of Line:** Douglas to Ramsey **Length of Line:** 5½ miles **Nº of Steam Locos:** None **Nº of Other Locos:** 3 vintage units **Approx Nº of Visitors P.A.:** 140,000 **Website:** www.rail.im

GENERAL INFORMATION

Nearest Mainline Station: Not applicable
Car Parking: Limited parking at all stations
Coach Parking: Available at Port Erin
Souvenir Shop(s): Souvenirs are available from all manned stations and from the shop at Port Erin Railway Museum
Food & Drinks: Yes – Douglas & Port Erin stations

SPECIAL INFORMATION

The Isle of Man Steam Railway is operated by the Isle of Man Government. A number of special events are held at the railway throughout the year.

OPERATING INFORMATION

Opening Times: 2024 dates: Most days from 29th March to 27th October but closed on Tuesdays and Wednesdays in April and October. Also closed on Tuesdays in May. Evening services operate during some of the summer months. Please contact the railway or check the web site for full details.
Steam Working: All scheduled services
Prices: Adult All-day Travel £19.00
   Child All-day Travel £9.50
   Family All-day Travel £42.00
Note: Lower prices are available for other journeys.

Detailed Directions:
By Sea from Heysham (Lancashire) or Liverpool to reach the Isle of Man. By Air from Belfast, Birmingham, Dublin, Glasgow, Gloucester, Jersey, Liverpool, Manchester, Newcastle, Bristol and London. Douglas Station is situated ½ mile inland from the Sea Terminal at the end of North Quay.

SNOWDON MOUNTAIN RAILWAY

Address: Llanberis, Caernarfon, Gwynedd, Wales LL55 4TY
Telephone Nº: (01286) 870223
Fax Nº: (01286) 872518
Year Formed: 1894
Location of Line: Llanberis to the summit of Snowdon/Yr Wyddfa

Length of Line: 4¾ miles
Nº of Steam Locos: 4
Nº of Other Locos: 4
Approx Nº of Visitors P.A.: 140,000
Gauge: 2 feet 7½ inches
Website: www.snowdonrailway.co.uk
E-mail: info@snowdonrailway.co.uk

GENERAL INFORMATION

Nearest Mainline Station: Bangor (9 miles)
Nearest Bus Station: Caernarfon (7½ miles)
Car Parking: Llanberis Station car park – pay and display. Also other car parks nearby.
Coach Parking: As above, but space is very limited.
Souvenir Shop(s): Yes
Food & Drinks: Yes

SPECIAL INFORMATION

Britain's only public rack and pinion railway climbs to within 60 feet of the 3,560 feet (1,085 metre) peak of Snowdon/Yr Wyddfa, the highest mountain in England and Wales.
The Diesel and Steam Experiences are both 2½ hour return journeys to the summit.

OPERATING INFORMATION

Opening Times: Open daily (weather permitting) from 23rd March to 27th October. Trains depart at regular intervals from 9.00am. The last departure can be as late as 5.30pm depending on demand. It is advisable to book in advance either online or by telephone to guarantee tickets.
Steam Working: Ride the "Snowdon Lily" or the "Mountain Goat" as part of the Heritage Steam Experience operating from May to September. Please contact the railway for further details.
Prices: Adult Summit Return £42.00 (Diesel)
Adult Summit Return £55.00 (Steam)
Child Summit Return £32.00 (Diesel)
Child Summit Return £45.00 (Steam)
Note: Until 14th May trains only travel up as far as Clogwyn, ¾ of the way up the mountain.

Detailed Directions by Car:
Llanberis Station is situated on the A4086 Caernarfon to Capel Curig road, 7½ miles from Caernarfon. Convenient access via the main North Wales coast road (A55). Exit at the A55/A5 junction and follow signs to Llanberis via B4366, B4547 and A4086.

SOUTH DOWNS LIGHT RAILWAY

Address: South Downs Light Railway, Stopham Road, Pulborough RH20 1DS	**Nº of Steam Locos:** 7
Telephone Nº: 07518 753784	**Nº of Other Locos:** 2
Year Formed: 1999	**Approx Nº of Visitors P.A.:** 20,000
Location: Pulborough Garden Centre	**Gauge:** 10¼ inches
Length of Line: 1 kilometre	**Website:** www.south-downs-railway.com
	E-mail: info@south-downs-railway.com

GENERAL INFORMATION

Nearest Mainline Station: Pulborough (½ mile)
Nearest Bus Station: Bus stop just outside Centre
Car Parking: Free parking on site
Coach Parking: Free parking on site
Souvenir Shop(s): Yes
Food & Drinks: Yes – in the Garden Restaurant

SPECIAL INFORMATION

The members of the Society own and operate a large collection of 10¼ inch gauge locomotives.
The Railway is located within the Pulborough Garden Centre.

OPERATING INFORMATION

Opening Times: Weekends and Bank Holidays from March until September, Wednesdays in School Holidays and also Santa Specials at weekends in December. Trains run from 11.00am to 3.30pm.
Steam Working: Most services are steam hauled.
Prices: Adult £2.50
Child £1.50 (Under-2s travel free)
Note: Supersaver tickets are also available and a special 'South Downs Belle' runs on the first Sunday of each month when fares cost an extra 50p.

Detailed Directions by Car:
From All Parts: The Centre is situated on the A283, ½ mile west of Pulborough. Pulborough itself is on the A29 London to Bognor Regis Road.

SOUTHEND PIER RAILWAY

Address: Western Esplanade, Southend-on-Sea SS1 1EE	**Nº of Steam Locos**: None
Telephone Nº: (01702) 212534	**Nº of Other Locos**: 2
Year Formed: 1889	**Approx Nº of Visitors P.A.**: 300,000
Location of Line: Southend seafront	**Gauge**: 3 feet
Length of Line: 2,180 yards	**Website**: www.southendpier.co.uk

GENERAL INFORMATION

Nearest Mainline Station: Southend Central (¼ mile)
Nearest Bus Station: Southend (¼ mile)
Car Parking: Available on the seafront
Coach Parking: Available
Souvenir Shop(s): Yes
Food & Drinks: Available

SPECIAL INFORMATION

The railway takes passengers to the end of Southend Pier which, at 1.33 miles, is the longest pleasure pier in the world.

OPERATING INFORMATION

Opening Times: Most days except for Christmas Day and on Mondays and Tuesdays during the winter months when the pier itself is closed. Trains run half-hourly.
Steam Working: None.
Prices: Adult Return £6.20
          Child Return £3.10
          Concessionary Return £3.10
          Family Return Ticket £16.00

Detailed Directions by Car:
From All Parts: Take the A127 to Southend and follow the brown tourist signs to the Pier.

SOUTH TYNEDALE RAILWAY

Address: The Railway Station, Alston, Cumbria CA9 3JB	**No of Steam Locos:** 4
Telephone No: (01434) 338214	**No of Other Locos:** 4
Year Formed: 1973	**Approx No of Visitors P.A.:** 22,000
Location of Line: From Alston, northwards along South Tyne Valley to Slaggyford	**Gauge:** 2 feet
Length of Line: 5 miles	**Web:** www.south-tynedale-railway.org.uk
	E-mail: enquiries@south-tynedale-railway.org.uk

GENERAL INFORMATION

Nearest Mainline Station: Haltwhistle (15 miles)
Nearest Bus Stop: Alston Townfoot (¼ mile)
Car Parking: Free parking at Alston Station but limited spaces available at Lintley & Slaggyford
Coach Parking: Free parking at Alston & Slaggyford Stations but a drop off point only at Lintley
Souvenir Shop(s): At Alston & Slaggyford Stations
Food & Drinks: Available at Alston & Slaggyford Stations

SPECIAL INFORMATION

The railway runs along part of the old Alston to Haltwhistle branch line in the South Tyne Valley.

OPERATING INFORMATION

Opening Times: 2024 dates: Bank Holidays and most weekends from 29th March to 27th October and also most days during the School Holidays. Please check the railway's website for information about other running dates for Special Events including Santa Specials.
Steam Working: Please contact the railway for details.
Prices: Adult Day Rover £16.00
Child Day Rover £8.00 (Under-3s free)
Dogs £2.00

Detailed Directions by Car:
Alston can be reached by a number of roads from various directions including A689, A686 and the B6277. Alston Station is situated just off the A686 Hexham road, north of Alston Town Centre. Look for the brown tourist signs on roads into Alston. Slaggyford Station is signposted off the A689.

STEEPLE GRANGE LIGHT RAILWAY

Address: Old Porter Lane, Steeple Grange, Wirksworth   DE4 4GE
Telephone Nº: (01629) 55123 (Evenings)
Year Formed: 1986
Location of Line: Adjacent to the High Peak trail near Wirksworth
Length of Line: ½ mile at present

Nº of Steam Locos: None
Nº of Other Locos: 11
Approx Nº of Visitors P.A.: 8,000+
Gauge: 18 inches
Website: www.sglr.co.uk

GENERAL INFORMATION

Nearest Mainline Station: Cromford (2 miles)
Nearest Bus Station: Matlock
Car Parking: Free parking in Old Porter Lane, plus other Pay and Display car parks nearby.
Coach Parking: Available nearby
Souvenir Shop(s): Yes
Food & Drinks: Light refreshments available

SPECIAL INFORMATION

The Railway is built on the track bed of the former Standard Gauge Cromford and High Peak Railway branch to Middleton. The railway uses mostly former mining/quarrying rolling stock and has two separate lines operating.

OPERATING INFORMATION

Opening Times: Sundays and Bank Holidays from the end of March until the end of September. Open on Saturdays in July and August and on other days by prior arrangement. Special Events run at other times of the year including Santa Specials during December. Please contact the railway for further information. Trains run from 12.00pm to 4.30pm
Steam Working: None
Prices: Adult Return £5.00   Child Return £3.00
        Senior Citizen Return £4.00
        Family Return £15.00
Note: Special fares apply during special events and also for group bookings.

Detailed Directions by Car:
The Railway is situated adjacent to the National Stone Centre just to the north of Wirksworth at the junction of the B5035 and B5036.

SUTTON HALL RAILWAY

Address: Tabors Farm, Sutton Hall, Shopland Road, near Rochford, Essex SS4 1LH
Telephone Nº: 07947 280573
Year Formed: 1997
Location of Line: Sutton Hall Farm
Length of Line: Almost 1 mile

Nº of Steam Locos: 1
Nº of Other Locos: 1
Approx Nº of Visitors P.A.: 3,500
Gauge: 10¼ inches
Website:
www.sutton-hall-railway.businesssite

GENERAL INFO

Nearest Mainline Station:
Southend Airport (2 miles)
Nearest Bus Station: Rochford
Car Parking:
Free parking available on site
Coach Parking:
Free parking available on site
Souvenir Shop(s): None
Food & Drinks:
Drinks and snacks available

SPECIAL INFORMATION

The Railway was bought by C. Tabor in 1985 for use with his Farm Barn Dances. The Sutton Hall Railway Society was formed in 1997 (with C. Tabor as Society President) and now opens the line for public running on some Sundays. The railway is staffed entirely by Volunteer Members of the Society.

OPERATING INFO

Opening Times: Open the 4th Sunday in the month from April until September, 12.00pm to 4.00pm. Also open on Easter Sunday 12.00pm to 4.00pm and the first Sunday in December, 12.00pm to 4.00pm.
Steam Working: All operating days.
Prices: Adults £2.50 per ride
Children £2.00 per ride
Note: The railway is also available to hire for private events.

Detailed Directions by Car:
From Southend Airport (A127 Southend to London Main Route & A1159): At the Airport Roundabout (with the McDonalds on the left) go over the railway bridge signposted for Rochford. At the 1st roundabout turn right (Ann Boleyn Pub on the right) into Sutton Road. Continue straight on at the mini-roundabout then when the road forks turn left into Shopland Road signposted for Barling and Great Wakering. Turn right after approximately 400 yards into the long tree-lined road for Sutton Hall Farm.

TALYLLYN RAILWAY

Address: Wharf Station, Tywyn, Gwynedd, LL36 9EY
Telephone Nº: (01654) 710472
Year Formed: 1865
Location of Line: Tywyn to Nant Gwernol
Length of Line: 7¼ miles

Nº of Steam Locos: 6
Nº of Other Locos: 4
Approx Nº of Visitors P.A.: 40,000
Gauge: 2 feet 3 inches
Website: www.talyllyn.co.uk
E-mail: enquiries@talyllyn.co.uk

GENERAL INFORMATION

Nearest Mainline Station: Tywyn (300 yards)
Nearest Bus Station: Tywyn (300 yards)
Car Parking: 100 yards away
Coach Parking: Free parking (100 yards)
Souvenir Shop(s): Yes
Food & Drinks: Yes

SPECIAL INFORMATION

Talyllyn Railway was the first preserved railway in the world – saved from closure in 1951. The railway was originally opened in 1866 to carry slate from Bryn Eglwys Quarry to Tywyn. Among the railway's attractions are a Narrow Gauge Railway Museum at the Tywyn Wharf terminus.
Find us on facebook and twitter!

OPERATING INFORMATION

Opening Times: 2024 dates: Daily from 23rd March to 3rd November. Also open on other selected dates in December for Santa Trains. Generally open from 10.30am to 5.00pm. Please contact the railway or check their web site for further details.
Steam Working: All services are steam-hauled.
Prices: Adult £25.40
          Child £12.70 (ages 5-15)
Children under the age of 5 travel free of charge.
Note: The prices shown are for Explorer tickets though passengers are encouraged to consider paying for slightly more expensive Gift Aid tickets.

Detailed Directions by Car:
From the North: Take the A493 from Dolgellau into Tywyn; From the South: Take the A493 from Machynlleth to Tywyn.

TEIFI VALLEY RAILWAY

Address: Henllan Station, Henllan, Llandysul SA44 5TD
Telephone Nº: (01559) 371077
Year Formed: 1978
Location of Line: Between Cardigan and Carmarthen off the A484
Length of Line: A third of a mile at present (in the process of being extended)

Nº of Steam Locos: 2
Nº of Other Locos: 3
Approx Nº of Visitors P.A.: 15,000
Gauge: 2 feet
Website: www.teifivalleyrailway.wales
E-mail: info@teifivalleyrailway.wales

GENERAL INFORMATION

Nearest Mainline Station: Carmarthen (10 miles)
Nearest Bus Station: Carmarthen (10 miles)
Car Parking: Spaces for 70 cars available.
Coach Parking: Spaces for 4 coaches available.
Souvenir Shop(s): Yes
Food & Drinks: Yes – Cafe is open on weekends

SPECIAL INFORMATION

The Railway was formerly part of the G.W.R. but now runs on a Narrow Gauge using Quarry Engines.

OPERATING INFORMATION

Opening Times: 2024 dates: Open daily from 7th to 28th April then every Wednesday and Sunday until the 8th September. Also open daily from 26th May to 2nd June and from 14th July to 8th September. Santa Specials operate on dates during December. Please contact the railway for further details. Trains run from 11.30am to 3.30pm.
Steam Working: Most operating days – please phone the Railway for further details.
Prices: Adult £5.00
Child £5.00

Detailed Directions by Car:
From All Parts: The Railway is situated in the Village of Henllan between the A484 and the A475 (on the B4334) about 4 miles east of Newcastle Emlyn.

THRELKELD QUARRY RAILWAY

Address: Threlkeld Quarry & Mining Museum, Threlkeld, Near Keswick, CA12 4TT
Telephone Nº: (01768) 779747
Year Formed: 2010
Website: www.threlkeldquarryandminingmuseum.co.uk
E-mail: quarryrailway@gmail.com

Nº of Steam Locos: 1   **Other Locos:** 2
Approx Nº of Visitors P.A.: 20,000
Gauge: 2 feet
Location of Line: Cumbria
Length of Line: ½ mile

GENERAL INFORMATION

Nearest Mainline Station:
Penrith (14 miles)
Nearest Bus Station:
Keswick (5 miles)
Car Parking: Available on site
Coach Parking: Available
Souvenir Shop(s): Yes
Food & Drinks: Available

SPECIAL INFORMATION

Underground tours (over-5s only) are available for an extra charge. Demonstration Working Weekends in conjunction with the Vintage Excavator Trust are held on the third weekend in May and September.

OPERATING INFO

Opening Times: 2024 dates: Daily from 29th March to the end of October half-term except for Mondays during School term time. Santa Specials also run on dates in December.
Please contact the Museum for details. Open from 10.00am to 5.00pm.
Steam Working: During the School Holidays and on Bank Holiday weekends. A Steam Gala is held on the last weekend in July.
Prices: Adult Museum
 Entry & Rides £9.00
 Child Museum
 Entry & Rides £5.00
 Concessions £8.50
An Annual Family Passes cost £45.00 to £64.00 depending on the numbers in the family.

Detailed Directions by Car:
From All Parts: Exit the M6 at Junction 40 and take the A66 towards Keswick. Turn off onto the B5322 at Threlkeld and follow signs for the Mining Museum.

TODDINGTON NARROW GAUGE RAILWAY

Address: The Station, Toddington, Cheltenham, Gloucestershire GL54 5DT
Telephone Nº: (01242) 621405
Year Formed: 1985
Gauge: 2 feet
Website: www.toddington-narrow-gauge.co.uk
E-mail: toddington.ngr@gmail.com

Location of Line: 5 miles south of Broadway, Worcestershire, near the A46
Length of Line: ½ mile
Nº of Steam Locos: 4
Nº of Other Locos: 7

GENERAL INFORMATION

Nearest Mainline Station: Cheltenham Spa or Ashchurch
Nearest Bus Station: Cheltenham
Car Parking: Parking available at Toddington
Coach Parking: Parking available as above
Souvenir Shop(s): None
Food & Drinks: None at the TNGR itself but available at the adjacent GWSR site.

SPECIAL INFORMATION

The railway is situated in the car park of Toddington Station on the Gloucestershire Warwickshire Railway.

OPERATING INFORMATION

Opening Times: 2024 dates: Most Sundays and Bank Holidays from 26th May to 8th September inclusive and also on most Saturdays in May. A number of Special Event weekends operate throughout the season. Please check the railway's website for details. Trains usually run every 35 minutes from 11.45am to 3.50pm.
Steam Working: Please check the website for further information.
Prices: Adults £5.00
            Children £2.00 (Under-5s ride free)

Detailed Directions by Car:
Toddington is 11 miles north east of Cheltenham, 5 miles south of Broadway just off the B4632 (old A46). Exit the M5 at Junction 9 towards Stow-on-the-Wold for the B4632. The Railway is clearly visible from the B4632.

VALE OF RHEIDOL RAILWAY

Address: Park Avenue, Aberystwyth,
Ceredigion SY23 1PG
Telephone Nº: (01970) 625819
Year Formed: 1897 (Opened in 1902)
Location: Aberystwyth to Devil's Bridge
Length of Line: 11¾ miles

Nº of Steam Locos: 6 (3 in regular service)
Nº of Other Locos: 1
Gauge: 1 foot 11¾ inches
Website: www.rheidolrailway.co.uk
E-mail: info@rheidolrailway.co.uk

GENERAL INFORMATION

Nearest Mainline Station: Aberystwyth (adjacent)
Nearest Bus Station: Aberystwyth (adjacent)
Car Parking: Available on site
Coach Parking: Parking available on site
Souvenir Shops: At Devil's Bridge and Aberystwyth
Food & Drinks: At Devil's Bridge and Aberystwyth

SPECIAL INFORMATION

The journey between the stations take one hour in
each direction. At Devil's Bridge there is a cafe,
toilets, a picnic area and the famous Mynach Falls.
The line climbs over 600 feet in 11¾ miles. Look out
for the Red Kites and Buzzards flying overhead!
"Driver for a Fiver" operates at Devil's Bridge on
certain days during the summer months.

OPERATING INFORMATION

Opening Times: 2024 dates: Services run daily
from 23rd March to 3rd November. Santa Trains
operate on dates during December. Please check the
web site or phone the railway for further details.
Steam Working: All trains are steam-hauled.
Prices: Adult Return £38.50
                    Child Return £5.50 (Under-3s ride free)
Note: Trains can be chartered by arrangement at
other times of the year. Please e-mail for details.

Detailed Directions by Car:
From the North take A487 into Aberystwyth. From the East take A470 and A44 to Aberystwyth. From the South
take A487 or A485 to Aberystwyth. The Station is located in the centre of town near the 'Park and Ride' site.
Follow the brown tourist signs from the edge of town.

VOLKS ELECTRIC RAILWAY

Address: Arch 285, Madeira Drive, Brighton BN2 1EN
Telephone Nº: (01273) 292718
Year Formed: 1883
Location of Line: Brighton seafront
Length of Line: 1 mile

Nº of Steam Locos: None
Nº of Other Locos: 7
Approx Nº of Visitors P.A.: 250,000
Gauge: 2 feet 8½ inches
Website: www.volksrailway.org.uk

GENERAL INFORMATION

Nearest Mainline Station: Brighton (2 miles)
Nearest Bus Station: Brighton Pier (¼ mile)
Car Parking: Available on site
Coach Parking: Available
Souvenir Shop(s): Yes
Food & Drinks: Available

SPECIAL INFORMATION

Opened in 1883, Volk's Electric Railway is the world's oldest operating electric railway. The brainchild of inventor Magnus Volk, the railway runs for just over a mile along Brighton seafront between Aquarium (for Brighton Pier) and Black Rock (for the Marina).

OPERATING INFORMATION

Opening Times: 2024 dates: Open daily from 29th March to 1st September, usually from 10.15am to 5.00pm. Services run until 6.00pm on weekends and Bank Holidays.
Steam Working: None
Prices: Adult Return £6.20 (Single £4.80)
Child Return £3.85 (Single £3.00)
Concession Return £4.80 (Single £3.40)
Family Return £16.10 (Single £11.80)

Detailed Directions by Car:
From All Parts: Take the A23/A27 to Brighton. The railway is located on the seafront next to the Pier and Wheel.

WATFORD MINIATURE RAILWAY

Address: Cassiobury Park, Watford, WD17 7LB
Telephone Nº: (01525) 854609
Year Formed: 1959
Location: At the northern end of Cassiobury Park, Watford
Length of Line: 1000 yards

Nº of Steam Locos: 3
Nº of Other Locos: 3
Approx Nº of Visitors P.A.: Not known
Gauge: 10¼ inches
Website: www.watfordrailway.co.uk
E-mail: watford@minirail.co.uk

GENERAL INFORMATION

Nearest Mainline Station: Watford Junction (appoximately 1½ miles)
Nearest Tube Station: Watford (400 yards)
Car Parking: Limited spaces available at the Park.
Coach Parking: None
Souvenir Shop(s): None
Food & Drinks: Cafe available in the Park.

OPERATING INFORMATION

Opening Times: 2024 dates: Weekends and School Holidays from January to November inclusive and daily from 29th June to 28th September. Also open in December for Santa Trains and during the first week in January. Open between 11.00am and 5.00pm throughout most of the year but from 12.00pm to 4.00pm in January, February and from late October to the end of the year.
Please check the web site for further information.
Steam Working: To be confirmed.
Steam running dates will be shown on the website.
Prices: All fares: £2.50 per ride (Under-2s free)

Detailed Directions by Car:
Exit the M25 at Junction 19 or 20 and follow the A41 to Watford. Turn right at the Dome Roundabout heading southwards on the A412 St. Albans Road and continue through Watford Town Centre onto the A412 Rickmansworth Road. Turn right onto Cassiobury Park Avenue, following the brown information sign and continue to the end of the road for the car park.

WAVENEY VALLEY RAILWAY

Address: Bressingham Steam Museum, Bressingham, Diss, Norfolk   IP22 2AA
Telephone No: (01379) 686900
Year Formed: Mid 1950's
Location of Line: Bressingham, Near Diss
Length of Line: 5 miles in total (3 lines)

No of Steam Locos: Many Steam locos of different gauges
Approx No of Visitors P.A.: 80,000+
Gauge: Standard, 2 foot, 10¼ inches and 15 inches
Website: www.bressingham.co.uk
E-mail: info@bressingham.co.uk

GENERAL INFORMATION

Nearest Mainline Station: Diss (2½ miles)
Nearest Bus Station: Bressingham (1¼ miles)
Car Parking: Free parking for 100 cars available
Coach Parking: Free parking for 30 coaches
Souvenir Shop(s): Yes
Food & Drinks: Yes

SPECIAL INFORMATION

In addition to Steam locomotives, Bressingham has a large selection of steam traction engines, fixed steam engines plus Dad's Army Exhibits and 17 acres of gardens.

OPERATING INFORMATION

Opening Times: 2024 dates: Daily from 28th March to 3rd November. Open from 10.30am to 5.00pm
Steam Working: Every operating day except for Mondays and Tuesdays outside the school holidays. Please contact the Museum for further details.
Prices: Adult £13.99 (non-Steam) £18.15 (Steam)
  Child £8.99 (non-Steam) £11.99 (Steam)
Note: Reduced entry charges are available for visitors who do not take railway rides.
The prices shown include a voluntary Gift Aid donation & online bookings are cheaper.

Detailed Directions by Car:
From All Parts: Take the A11 to Thetford and then follow the A1066 towards Diss for Bressingham. The Museum is signposted by the brown tourist signs.   SATNAV please use the following post code: IP22 2AA

WELLINGTON COUNTRY PARK RAILWAY

Address: Odiham Road, Riseley, RG7 1SP
Telephone Nº: (0118) 932-6444
Year Formed: 1980
Location of Line: Riseley, Berkshire
Length of Line: 500 yards
Website: www.wellingtoncountrypark.co.uk

Nº of Steam Locos: None
Nº of Other Locos: 1
Approx Nº of Visitors P.A.: 140,000+ (to the Country Park)
Gauge: 12¼ inches
E-mail: countryparkinfo@wellington.co.uk

GENERAL INFORMATION

Nearest Mainline Station: Mortimer (5 miles)
Nearest Bus Station: Reading (9 miles)
Car Parking: Available on site
Coach Parking: Available
Souvenir Shop(s): Yes
Food & Drinks: Available

SPECIAL INFORMATION

The railway is located within 350 acres of beautiful parklands which surround a 35 acre lake. The line itself has recently been converted from a 7¼ inch gauge to a 12¼ inch gauge.

OPERATING INFORMATION

Opening Times: 2024 dates: Daily from mid-February until 3rd November. Open from 9.30am to 5.30pm (but until 4.30pm during the Winter).
Steam Working: None
Prices: Adults £19.95 (Park Admission)
Children £19.95 (Park Admission)
Under-2s are admitted free of charge
Note: Prices shown are for High Season admissions and tickets must be pre-booked for a particular entry-time slot.

Detailed Directions by Car:
From All Parts: Exit the M4 at Junction 11 and take the A33 towards Basingstoke. Turn onto the B3349 at the Riseley roundabout and follow the signs to the Park which is straight off the roundabout.

WELLS & WALSINGHAM LIGHT RAILWAY

Address: Stiffkey Road, Wells-next-the-Sea, NR23 1QB
Telephone Nº: (01328) 711630
Year Formed: 1982
Location of Line: Wells-next-the-Sea to Walsingham, Norfolk
Length of Line: 4 miles

Nº of Steam Locos: 2
Nº of Other Locos: 2
Approx Nº of Visitors P.A.: 33,000
Gauge: 10¼ inches
Website: www.wwlr.co.uk

GENERAL INFORMATION

Nearest Mainline Station: King's Lynn (21 miles)
Nearest Bus Station: Norwich (24 miles)
Car Parking: Parking at site
Coach Parking: Parking at site
Souvenir Shop(s): Yes

SPECIAL INFORMATION

The Railway is the longest 10¼ inch narrow-gauge steam railway in the world. The course of the railway is famous for wildlife and butterflies in season.

OPERATING INFORMATION

Opening Times: 2024 dates: Daily from 23rd March until 3rd November.
Steam Working: Most operating days with a diesel service on Mondays except for during the school holidays. Trains run from 10.30am on most days (10.00am during the school summer holidays).
Prices: Adult Return £12.50
Child Return £9.50 (Under-4s ride free)
Family Return £40.00

Detailed Directions by Car:
Wells-next-the-Sea is situated on the North Norfolk Coast midway between Hunstanton and Cromer. The Main Station is situated on the main A149 Stiffkey Road. Follow the brown tourist signs for the Railway.

WELSH HIGHLAND HERITAGE RAILWAY

Address: Tremadog Road, Porthmadog, Gwynedd LL49 9DY
Telephone Nº: (01766) 513402
Year Formed: 1961
Location of Line: Opposite Porthmadog Mainline Station
Length of Line: 1½ mile round trip

Nº of Steam Locos: 5
Nº of Other Locos: 19
Approx Nº of Visitors P.A.: 25,000
Gauge: 1 foot 11½ inches
Website: www.whr.co.uk
E-mail: info@whr.co.uk

GENERAL INFORMATION

Nearest Mainline Station: Porthmadog (adjacent)
Nearest Bus Station: Services 1 & 3 stop 50 yards away
Car Parking: Free parking at site, plus a public Pay and Display car park within 100 yards
Coach Parking: Adjacent
Souvenir Shop(s): Yes – large range available
Food & Drinks: Yes – excellent home cooking at the Russell Team Room!

SPECIAL INFORMATION

The Welsh Highland Railway is a family-orientated attraction based around a Railway Heritage Centre and includes a guided, hands-on tour of the sheds.

OPERATING INFORMATION

Opening Times: 2024 dates: Daily from 25th March to 14th April, then most weekends, Wednesdays and Thursdays from May to 20th July.
Open daily from 20th July to 1st September then weekends and Thursdays in October.
Steam Working: Most days during the School Holidays and on other selected weekends.
Please check with the railway for further details.
Prices: Adult Day Rover £12.75
Child Day Rover £6.00 (Under-3s free)
Family Day Rover £34.00
(2 adults + 2 children)

Detailed Directions by Car:
From Bangor/Caernarfon take the A487 to Porthmadog. From Pwllheli take the A497 to Porthmadog then turn left at the roundabout. From the Midlands take A487 to Portmadog. Once in Porthmadog, follow the brown tourist signs. The line is located right next to Porthmadog Mainline Station, opposite the Queens Hotel.

WELSH HIGHLAND RAILWAY

Postal Address: Ffestiniog Railway, Harbour Station, Porthmadog LL49 9NF	**Nº of Steam Locos:** 8 (5 working)
Telephone Nº: (01766) 516000	**Nº of Other Locos:** 3
Year Formed: 1997	**Approx Nº of Visitors P.A.:** 360,000
Location: Caernarfon to Porthmadog	**Gauge:** 1 foot 11½ inches
Length of Line: 25 miles	**Website:** www.festrail.co.uk
	E-mail: enquiries@festrail.co.uk

GENERAL INFORMATION

Nearest Mainline Station: Porthmadog (½ mile), Bangor (7 miles) (Bus service Nº 5 to Caernarfon)
Nearest Bus Station: Porthmadog or Caernarfon
Car Parking: Parking available at Caernarfon
Coach Parking: At Victoria Docks (¼ mile from Caernarfon station) and in Porthmadog
Souvenir Shop(s): Yes
Food & Drinks: A full buffet is available on most trains.

SPECIAL INFORMATION

The Railway has been reconstructed between Caernarfon and Porthmadog Harbour along the track bed of the original Welsh Highland Railway.

2011 saw the completion of this spectacular route passing from coast to coast through the majestic scenery of the Snowdonia National Park.

OPERATING INFORMATION

Opening Times: 2024 dates: Daily from 29th March to 3rd November. A limited service also operates during the Winter and Santa Specials run on dates in December.
Steam Working: Most trains are steam hauled.
Prices: A variety of routes ranging between Blaenau Ffestiniog, Porthmadog and Caernarfon are available following the link-up with the Welsh Highland Railway, so please check the website for full details of the various fares.

Detailed Directions by Car:
Take either the A487(T), the A4085 or the A4086 to Caernarfon then follow the brown tourist signs for the Railway which is situated in St. Helens Road next to the Castle.

WELSHPOOL & LLANFAIR LIGHT RAILWAY

Address: The Station, Llanfair Caereinion, Powys SY21 0SF
Telephone N°: (01938) 810441
Year Formed: 1959
Location of Line: Welshpool to Llanfair Caereinion, Mid Wales
Length of Line: 8 miles

N° of Steam Locos: 7
N° of Other Locos: 5
Approx N° of Visitors P.A.: 26,000
Gauge: 2 feet 6 inches
Website: www.wllr.org.uk
E-mail: info@wllr.org.uk

GENERAL INFORMATION

Nearest Mainline Station: Welshpool (1 mile)
Nearest Bus Station: Welshpool (1 mile)
Car Parking: Free parking at Welshpool and Llanfair Caereinion
Coach Parking: As above
Souvenir Shop(s): Yes – at both ends of line
Food & Drinks: Yes – at Llanfair only

SPECIAL INFORMATION

The railway has the steepest gradient of any British adhesion railway (1 in 29) and reaches a summit of 603 feet.

OPERATING INFORMATION

Opening Times: 2024 dates: Most days from 23rd March to 29th September except for Fridays, Mondays and Tuesdays. Santa Specials operate on weekends and some Mondays in December. Trains usually run from 10.00am until 5.00pm.
Steam Working: Most trains are steam-hauled
Prices: Adult Day Rover £23.00
Child Day Rover £10.00 (Under-3s free)
Family Day Rovers £31.00 to £54.00
(Price depends on the number of Family members)

Detailed Directions by Car:
Both stations are situated alongside the A458 Shrewsbury to Dolgellau road and are clearly signposted

WEST LANCASHIRE LIGHT RAILWAY

Address: Station Road, Hesketh Bank, Nr. Preston, Lancashire PR4 6SP
Telephone N°: (01772) 815881
Year Formed: 1967
Location of Line: On former site of Alty's Brickworks, Hesketh Bank
Length of Line: ¼ mile

N° of Steam Locos: 5
N° of Other Locos: 23
Approx N° of Visitors P.A.: 10,000
Gauge: 2 feet
Website: www.westlancsrailway.org

GENERAL INFORMATION

Nearest Mainline Station: Preston (10 miles). Take the No. 2 bus outside the station.
Nearest Bus Station: Preston (10 miles). Take the No. 2 bus to Hesketh Bank Booths.
Car Parking: Space for 50 cars at site
Coach Parking: Space for 3 coaches at site
Souvenir Shop(s): Yes
Food & Drinks: Hot and cold drinks and snacks plus a catering van for hot fast food on Gala Days.

SPECIAL INFORMATION

The Railway is run by volunteers and there is a large collection of Industrial Narrow Gauge equipment.

OPERATING INFORMATION

Opening Times: 2024 dates: Sundays and Bank Holidays from 31st March to 3rd November. Santa Trains run in December. For details of other special events please check the website. Trains run from 11.30am to 5.00pm.
Steam Working: Trains operate on Sundays and Bank Holidays from April until the end of October.
Prices: Adult £4.00
         Child £3.00
         Family Tickets £13.00
         Senior Citizens £3.50
Note: Different fares apply for Gala Days and Santa Specials.

Detailed Directions by Car:
Travel by the A59 from Liverpool or Preston or by the A565 from Southport to the junction of the two roads at Tarleton. From here follow signs to Hesketh Bank. The Railway is signposted.

WINDMILL ANIMAL FARM RAILWAY

Address: Windmill Animal Farm, Fish Lane, Burscough L40 1UQ	**Nº of Steam Locos:** 4
Telephone Nº: (01704)892282	**Nº of Other Locos:** 10
Year Formed: 1997	**Approx Nº of Visitors P.A.:** 70,000 (with around 35,000 taking train rides)
Location of Line: Burscough, Lancashire	**Gauge:** 15 inches
Length of Line: 1 mile	**Website:** www.windmillanimalfarm.co.uk

GENERAL INFORMATION

Nearest Mainline Station: Burscough (2½ miles)
Nearest Bus Station: Southport (8½ miles)
Car Parking: Available at the Farm
Coach Parking: Available at the Farm
Souvenir Shop(s): Yes
Food & Drinks: Available

SPECIAL INFORMATION

In addition to the railway, the site includes a play area and a large number of farm animals with a petting area where children can feed the animals.

OPERATING INFORMATION

Opening Times: 2024 dates: Open daily from the beginning of February until December when Santa Specials operate.
Trains run from 11.00am to 4.00pm.
Steam Working: Every weekend
Prices: Adult Admission £14.95
Child Admission £15.95
Concession Admission £12.95
Train Rides: The prices shown include both admission to the farm and train rides.

Detailed Directions by Car:
From All Parts: Exit the M6 at Junction 27 and take the A5209 following signs for Southport. On entering Burscough follow signs for Burscough Bridge and Martin Lane. Turn left into Red Cat Lane just by Burscough Bridge train station and follow the road along for Windmill Animal Farm and the Railway.